BRIGHT IDEAS

Timesa

Written by Lynda Smith

Published by Scholastic Publications Ltd,
Villiers House, Clarendon Avenue,
Leamington Spa, Warwickshire CV32 5PR

© 1991 Scholastic Publications Ltd

Written by Lynda Smith
Edited by Juliet Gladston
Sub-edited by Catherine Baker
Illustrated by Lynda Smith and
Lesley Smith

Printed in Great Britain by
Loxley Brothers Ltd, Sheffield.

**British Library Cataloguing in Publication
Data**
Smith, Lynda
    Bright ideas: timesavers
    1. Primary schools. Teaching
    I. Title
    372.1102

    ISBN 0-590-76432-2

Front and back cover designed by Sue Limb
Photographed by Martyn Chillmaid

Contents

Introduction

The essence of this book is timesaving. It is aimed at busy teachers and is designed to save time by eliminating unnecessary preparation by providing material which can be photocopied and used for a variety of purposes. Each chapter contains a selection of relevant photocopiable pages in conjunction with concise back-up information giving examples of how to use each page, and additional background information where required.

Frequently needed forms, letters, charts, outlines and designs are all provided – some of which are specific to certain events and others which can be used in a more general way; for example, as decoration. All the pages can easily be adapted to suit particular needs, but best of all they dispense with the need to spend time in designing and drawing out your own originals.

PHOTOCOPYING

To use this book most effectively, it is vital that you have easy access to a photocopier. Photocopiers have become everyday objects in most schools and are in themselves economic with time, although every machine seems to have its own characteristics and foibles. There are some simple guides, however, which apply to all machines and will help to keep photocopying quick and trouble-free.
● Never make copies too dark as excessive darkness will make the copies appear foggy.
● Only copy one sheet at a time until you are happy with the reproduction.
● Use a blank sheet of paper to cover any sections of the sheet you do not wish to photocopy. If this is not practical, photocopy

the whole sheet, cut out what is wanted and stick it in place on a new sheet of paper. Ensure that the edges are stuck down firmly so that there is less risk of a shadow of the outline appearing.
● Do not forget that copies can be made on some types of acetate film, so that material can be used on an overhead projector.

ABOUT THIS BOOK

Each chapter in this book covers a different area of school life. The first chapter, 'Behaviour and rewards', includes lots of material to help in the positive reinforcement of good work and attitudes, for example, by providing certificates and messages home. It also offers material for when all is not well, for example, behaviour and work contracts, and incident sheets. Also, there are a number of personal profile sheets which the children can use themselves to express their worries and feelings.

The chapters 'The classroom' and 'School administration' provide a range of ideas and items that should prove useful in organising and running the classroom or school. It includes labels, timetables, reading records, book reviews, charts and map outlines, as well as material which can be used by the children in conjunction with lots of different topics.

The chapter on 'Parent liaison and school events' gives designs for handbills to advertise school events such as a Book Week, and provides a proforma for a sponsorship form, as well as giving ideas to encourage parent helpers, checklists for parents and information for parents on healthy food and road safety.

The final chapter looks at 'Special occasions'. It gives photocopiable material which can be used for a multitude of purposes for festivals and celebrations throughout the year. It also provides some concise information on the background to each celebration. Obviously, not all occasions can be covered but many of the most popular festivals and the five main religions are represented.

Behaviour and rewards

Behaviour record sheets

Age range
Sheet 1: Four to seven.
Sheet 2: Seven to eleven.

Group size
Individuals.

What you need
Photocopiable page 15 or 16, depending on the age range of the children.

What to do
Often, when a child is frequently disruptive or has unacceptable modes of behaviour, such as shouting or aggression, many of the usual disciplinary actions fail in the long term. One way of trying to keep acceptable behaviour at the forefront of a child's mind, is to use a behaviour record sheet.

It is important to explain to the child what behaviour modifications are required, and the purpose of the sheet. Behaviour should be assessed at the end of each of the four daily sessions and then the child can add an appropriate facial expression to the appropriate face on the chart. For example, a smile could indicate that the child behaved in the manner agreed, while a sad expression would mean that the child failed to behave correctly. Initially, try not to be too stringent or rigid. Be positive and patient and give the idea time to work.

The principle for both photocopiable pages is the same, but page 16 is aimed to appeal to older children. Although the older child needs the same positive approach, the incentives used may need to be greater. This depends very much on the individual child and the

organisation of the school. Are there particularly prized 'jobs' in school that could be the ultimate goal after an agreed period of good behaviour?

If you think the rest of the class are able to help in improving a particular child's behaviour, then try to involve them too, but be careful how you do this. They should be encouraged to praise good behaviour and not to tell tales!

If parents are involved, make a space at the bottom of the form for them to sign when the child takes a photocopy home. Encourage them to praise their child when it is deserved.

This type of record often helps to improve behaviour and motivation, particularly when the child completes the sheet, and it can also serve as a useful record, forming part of a profile of a particularly difficult or disturbed child.

Playtime contracts

Age range
Sheet 1: Four to seven.
Sheet 2: Seven to eleven.

Group size
Individuals.

What you need
Photocopiable page 17 or 18, depending on the age range of the children.

What to do
Many children's behaviour is perfectly acceptable in the classroom, but degenerates as soon as they find themselves in the less restricted situation of the playground. Making a contract with a child may help him become more aware of his misconduct and give him the incentive to have more self-control. This type of sheet allows an agreement to be made between you and the child as to what behaviour is and is not wanted.

Photocopiable page 17 is designed for use with younger children and allows some flexibility in the way it is completed. For example, it can be filled in each day for each playtime, or completed once per day, with each column lasting a week. The form can be completed by you and/or the child, whichever seems applicable. Photocopiable page 18, for older children, provides space for both you and the child to record your opinion of the child's behaviour.

The space at the bottom of each sheet could be used for other comments or for the teacher on duty in the playground to sign.

Various ways of filling the appropriate square are possible, for example ticks, comments, facial expressions, stars and so on.

As with all these behaviour modification ideas, try to be positive, and give this approach a reasonable amount of time to take effect.

Feelings charts

Age range
Sheet 1: Four to seven.
Sheets 2 and 3: Seven to eleven.

Group size
Individuals.

What you need
Photocopiable page 19, 20 or 21, depending on the age range of the children.

What to do
Children who may have some behavioural difficulties and/or emotional problems usually need a lot of individual attention, sympathy and encouragement to enable them to express their feelings. However, in a busy classroom where time is a limited resource, it is often difficult to put aside the amount of time needed by these children. Therefore, photocopiable pages 19 to 21 offer a simple and relatively quick way of discovering the emotions and feelings of a child who may be having problems or whose actions are a cause for concern.

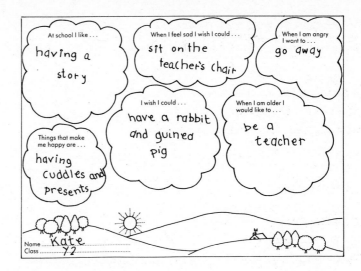

Apart from children who have long-term problems, sometimes children's behaviour seems to change suddenly for reasons that are not always immediately obvious. Here the feelings charts may help in giving some insight into the problems which caused the change of behaviour, and so allow for the correct help and support to be given.

Photocopiable page 19 is designed to be used by younger children. They should try to complete the facial expressions each day, and explain to the teacher how they feel and why. If they are capable, they can also write down their feelings and thoughts.

Photocopiable pages 20 and 21, for older children, can be completed with very little prompting. They provide children with a chance to give a personal and immediate response, which will hopefully give you some insight into their feelings, opinions and perplexities.

These charts can also be used in topic work, for example on themes such as 'Myself', 'Feelings' and 'Growing up'. They can give you quite a different perception of the children and provide useful feedback.

Incident records

Age range
Four to eleven.

Group size
Individuals.

What you need
Photocopiable page 22.

What to do
If a child's behaviour is causing enough concern to involve parents, then a record of misdemeanours kept over a period of time is a necessary and often convincing tool when tackling this sensitive problem. It is also an important record to pass on to other educational agencies, such as educational psychologists, when it is felt that help is needed from bodies outside the school.

Use photocopiable page 22 to record incidents involving either one or a number of children. Fill in the record as soon as possible after the incident and keep a file of incident sheets in each class or centrally, for example, in the headteacher's room. All staff, including lunchtime supervisors, should be involved in keeping these records.

These records should not be used as a threat to children – 'Behave, or you'll go in the Incident Book' – but should be kept confidential among staff and governors. Parents should only be shown the sheets relevant to their child.

Personal incident sheet

Age range
Seven to eleven.

Group size
Individuals or groups.

What you need
Photocopiable page 22.

What to do
When a child has been involved in an incident requiring further investigation and/or explanation, try using a personal incident sheet as shown on photocopiable page 22. Here the children involved can try to write their own version of the incident, with help if necessary from a member of staff or an older child.

These sheets often give further insight into an incident and its cause, and may bring to light deeper, underlying problems. It is useful to keep these sheets in a central folder for reference and as an aid if parents or other agencies need to be advised.

Date	Work title	Comments
1.8.91	Map of Scandinavia	Interesting. I liked using the atlas.
1.8.91	Viking sea routes	I learnt a lot. The Vikings were good sailors.
1.8.91	Balsa wood model of a longship	I love doing this
2.8.91	Writing like Vikings – Runes	I got a bit muddled.
2.8.91	A plan of a viking ship	Doing scale drawings is hard.

Work diary

Age range
Seven to eleven.

Group size
Individuals or groups.

What you need
Photocopiable page 23.

What to do
A work diary can be used as a way of encouraging less motivated children in their work. Each day the child should record the work she has done, together with her comments about what she felt about it. This can give you valuable feedback and enable you to evaluate the work being done in the classroom. Did the children enjoy the work? Was the work pitched at the right level for their abilities?

The diary can also be used as a regular part of classroom procedure for all children.

Work contracts

Age range
Six to eleven.

Group size
Individuals.

What you need
Photocopiable pages 24 and 25.

What to do
Work contracts do not only have to be used with children who fail to complete an acceptable amount of work; they can also be used in the normal routine of the classroom. Together with individuals or groups, you can decide what work or activities need to be completed or experienced over a period of time, and then work in the usual way. However, for children who are not completing an acceptable amount of work, the contract could also include an evaluation section in which the children can write their opinions, how difficult or easy they found the work, what new knowledge or skills they have discovered, and so on.

Decide on the best approach for each child involved. Should the contract cover all curriculum areas or are there specific areas that need targeting? Then simply agree with the child the work that will be attempted or completed, on either a daily or a weekly basis, and let the child fill in photocopiable page 24 or 25.

Ensure that on completion of the work the child is given plenty of praise and a concrete prize, such as team points. It is important to give the contract system a fair trial, as initially it may take some time to have an effect.

Experiment with variations, and try not to set the children's goals too high so that they have a good chance of experiencing success early on.

Messages home

Age range
Four to eleven.

Group size
Individuals.

What you need
Photocopiable page 26.

What to do
Most children respond well to praise, and if that praise is conveyed home the effects can be even greater.

Photocopiable page 26 provides two sheets which can be completed with a positive message, for example, praising a child's good work or caring attitude. These can then either be displayed in the school or a copy sent home. Both of these will raise self-esteem in any child.

This sharing of commendations not only benefits the child, but also helps to enhance the school's image and aids parent–teacher relationships.

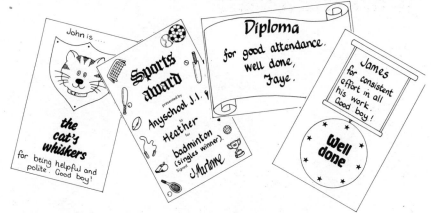

Certificates and diplomas

Age range
Four to eleven.

Group size
Individuals and groups.

What you need
Photocopiable pages 27 and 28.

What to do
Praising good work and rewarding effort by giving certificates and diplomas to children is another positive way of encouraging children. These certificates can be given within the classroom, or as part of a whole-school effort, for example, by having presentations in assembly.

The certificates and diplomas shown on pages 27 and 28 can be used as part of a reward after children have successfully completed work or behaviour contracts. They can be displayed centrally within the school, where other children and visitors can see them, or within the classroom, with copies sent home.

Stickers and badges

Age range
Four to eleven.

Group size
Individuals.

What you need
Photocopiable page 29, scissors, card, adhesive, sticky tape, safety-pin.

What to do
Being praised is important to all children, and rewarding them with stickers and badges gives them extra satisfaction.

Photocopiable page 29 can be used to make badges and stickers. The shapes can be coloured in, or you and the children can design your own using the blank shapes. To make them into badges stick them on to cardboard with adhesive and either stick a loop of sticky tape or a safety-pin on to the back of the card so that they can be attached to clothing. Stickers can be made by adding a loop of sticky tape to the back of the paper shapes or by using a paper adhesive. Both the badges and stickers can be covered with clear adhesive plastic to make them more durable.

The children could design their own booklets to keep their stickers in and could take these home regularly.

It is best not to be over-generous in giving out these rewards, in case they lose their 'special' quality. It is also important that all children manage to get a sticker occasionally. Obviously, some children will get more than others, but if some see them as impossible to gain, it could cause negative attitudes.

Behaviour record sheets, see page 7

Name..........................

Class..........................

Date..........................

Morning

Afternoon

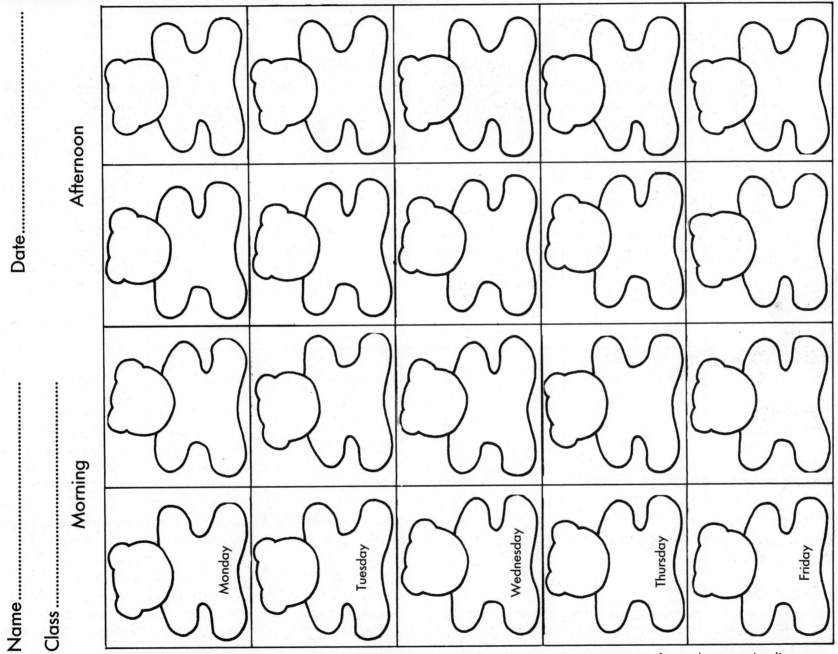

Monday

Tuesday

Wednesday

Thursday

Friday

Behaviour record sheets, see page 7

Name.. Class .... Date..

Session	Monday	Tuesday	Wednesday	Thursday	Friday
1					
2					
3					
4					

Pupil to add appropriate facial expression.

This page may be photocopied for use in the classroom and should not be declared in any return in respect of any photocopying licence.

16

Playtime contracts, see page 8

I agree to ....

....

Signed ....

	Playtime am		Lunchtime		Playtime pm	
	Pupil	Teacher	Pupil	Teacher		Teacher

Playtime contracts, see page 8

I am going to be well-behaved in the playground.

Signed ....

Date ....

Monday	Tuesday	Wednesday	Thursday	Friday

Feelings charts, see page 9

Today I feel......

Monday	Tuesday	Wednesday	Thursday	Friday

Feelings charts, see page 9

What makes me . . .

happy

sad

laugh

angry

scared

Feelings charts, see page 9

At school I like . . .

When I feel sad I wish I could . . .

When I am angry I want to . . .

I wish I could . . .

When I am older I would like to . . .

Things that make me happy are . . .

Name ....
Class ....

This page may be photocopied for use in the classroom and should not be declared in any return in respect of any photocopying licence.

Incident record

Date

Children involved

Details of incident

Action taken

Signed

Personal incident sheet

Date

Name

What happened to me

Signed

Class

This page may be photocopied for use in the classroom and should not be declared in any return in respect of any photocopying licence.

Work diary, see page 11

Date	Work title	Comments

Name.................... Class.................... Subject....................

Work contracts, see page 12

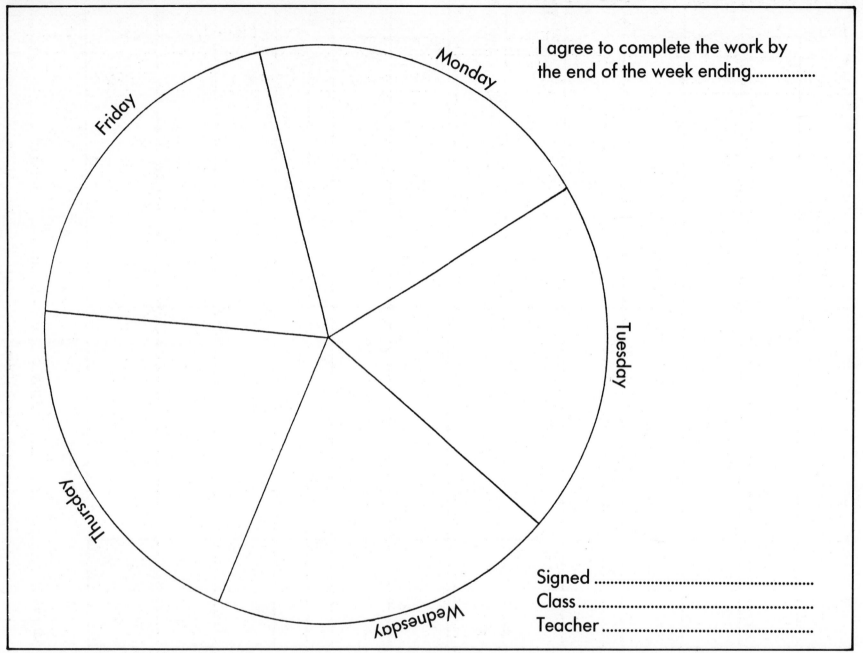

I agree to complete the work by the end of the week ending................

Monday

Tuesday

Wednesday

Thursday

Friday

Signed ....
Class ....
Teacher ....

Work contracts, see page 12

Name .... Class .... Signed...

Work contract	Monday	Tuesday	Wednesday	Thursday	Friday

My teacher says ....

....

....

....

....

....

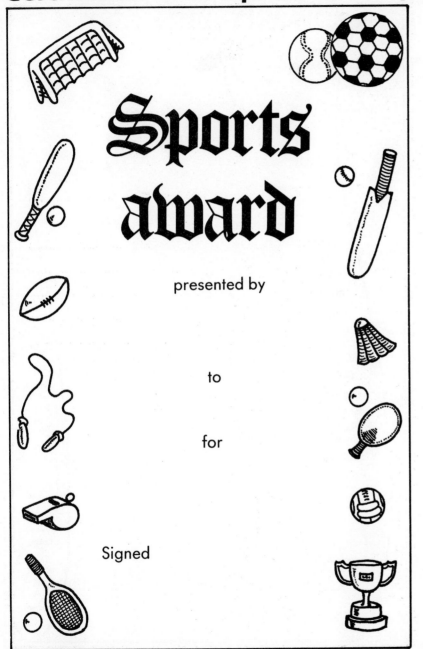

the
cat's
whiskers

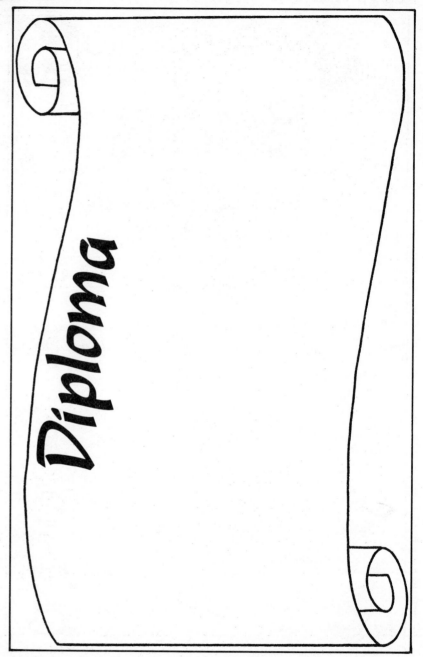

Teacher's award

Well read

I'm star pupil

For trying

I've sailed through my work

The classroom

Reading diary and record

Age range
Seven to eleven.

Group size
Individuals or groups.

What you need
Photocopiable pages 39 and 40.

What to do
Reading skills require ongoing assessment. Recording what children read is an integral part of this monitoring process, whereby children's reading experience, their enjoyment and progress can all be assessed.

The reading diary and record on pages 39 and 40 provide simple and flexible ways of recording the books read by the children, either at school or at home. The books may have been read silently, in a group or shared, and the sheets can be completed by you, the children and/or their parents.

The reading diary on photocopiable page 39 leaves space to fill in the date the book was finished, the title of the book and how much time was spent on it. The most important part is the area allowed for comments; here the children can say whether they enjoyed the book or not, whereas teachers can remark on such things as the child's confidence, fluency, intonation and effort.

The reading record on photocopiable page 40 is a simpler chart, having only two columns which can be used either to record the titles of books read over a two-week period or to record the titles of books read over one week, together with comments about them.

To encourage the children's interest in filling in these charts they can colour the illustrations and add further detail or drawings of their own.

Book reviews

Age range
Five to eleven.

Group size
Individuals.

What you need
Photocopiable pages 41 and 42.

What to do
Asking children to write reviews of books that they have read is an effective way to assess their comprehension levels, and their attitudes towards their reading material in general, as well as developing their critical skills.

Photocopiable pages 41 and 42 are designed so that they can easily be completed by the children for a book they have particularly enjoyed. Page 41 is intended to be used by younger children. They can write the title of the book they have read and their name on the teddy's hat and then complete the sentence 'I liked . . .', adding the name of a favourite character or part of the story. They can then colour the teddy on the sheet which they feel shows best how they feel about the book, or they can fill in the blank one and add their own adjective. Once the writing work has been completed, they can colour the large teddy.

Page 42 is intended to be used by older children as its completion requires both summation and evaluation skills. The children should fill in as much as they can of this sheet as soon as possible after having read a book.

Weather chart

Age range
Four to eleven.

Group size
Any.

What you need
Photocopiable page 43.

What to do
The topic of weather is an integral part of the primary curriculum which is often studied as part of a wider theme.

   The simple chart on photocopiable page 43 can be completed by individual children, by groups or by the whole class. Its simple format means that it is very flexible. Young children, for example, could draw pictures of the daily weather conditions or pictures of the clothes they need to wear, while older children could use standard weather symbols and add further data such as the temperature and humidity.

Week	Monday	Tuesday	Wednesday	Thursday	Friday
1	rain	sunny with showers	sunny	cloudy	cloudy
2	sunny and hot	sunny and hot	really hot	still hot	thunder
3	cloudy with some sunshine	sunny and warm			
4					
5					
6					

Growth chart

Age range
Six to eleven.

Group size
Any.

What you need
Photocopiable page 44.

What to do
Children often have to measure and record the growth of a seedling as part of a science or maths activity. The chart on photocopiable page 44 is intended to be a fun way for the children to plot the growth of a seed or cutting. As the plant grows the children can colour the ruler up to the appropriate measurement. There is also room for them to add the date each measurement was taken. The leaves on the illustrations can also be coloured as each new leaf appears on the seedling. Finally, extra sheets can be added if necessary so that the ruler is extended.

Blank grids and lined paper

Age range
Four to eleven.

Group size
Any.

What you need
Photocopiable pages 45, 46 and 47.

What to do
It is not always easy to find the types of lined and squared paper which are often needed in a busy classroom. Therefore, pages 45 to 47 provide a useful selection.

The lines on page 45 can be used by the children for practising their handwriting, writing letters and so on. Page 46 provides music staves for composing tunes or writing out music. The example of squared paper on page 47 provides a grid which can be used for graph work, tessellations, symmetry, area, recording data, rotas, board games, number work, addition, subtraction and table squares, plans, grid references, co-ordinates work . . . the scope is endless.

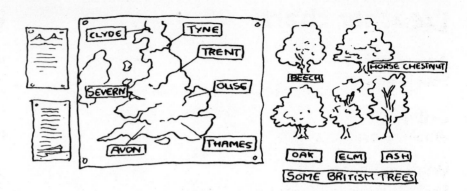

Map outlines

Age range
Seven to eleven.

Group size
Individuals or groups.

What you need
Photocopiable pages 48, 49 and 50.

What to do
Pre-drawn outlines of countries are obviously very helpful for children when studying countries or topics such as climate, industry and agriculture. They are very difficult for children to draw themselves and time consuming for you to draw out. However, most children are capable of adding various features to the outlines and colouring them in.

Photocopiable page 48 shows the outline of the United Kingdom with the Scottish, Welsh and Northern Irish boundaries marked. Page 49 shows the British Isles in relation to Europe and finally, page 50 shows the whole world.

Labels

Age range
Four to eleven.

Group size
Whole class.

What you need
Photocopiable pages 51 and 52, adhesive, scissors.

What to do
A well-labelled classroom helps make day-to-day classroom life easier for both you and the children. If equipment is clearly labelled, the children will be able to find and put away independently, any items they require and thereby save you having always to collect and tidy away equipment for them.

There are two different types of labels shown on photocopiable pages 51 and 52. The first set is pictorial; these are best used with younger children or less able readers. The second set uses words only, and these labels are therefore more appropriate for older children. On both pages there are blank copies which you can use to draw or write your own labels.

To use the labels, cut them out and cover them with clear self-adhesive plastic for durability. Stick them to the appropriate objects with adhesive or sticky tape. The children could colour them before cutting them out, or you could photocopy them using coloured paper.

Photograph album

Age range
Six to eleven.

Group size
Individuals.

What you need
Photocopiable page 53.

What to do
Page 53 represents a page from a photograph album. It can be used in a number of ways; for example, as a personal profile for a child, or as part of a topic such as 'Ourselves'. The children can add their own captions to the 'photographs' once they have drawn or stuck in pictures. If more specific information is needed, you can write the captions before the children add the pictures.

This simple sheet can provide a great deal of information about a child's likes and dislikes, social awareness and attitudes, and it may be useful to use this in conjunction with sheets in the 'Behaviour and rewards' chapter.

Passport

Age range
Eight to eleven.

Group size
Individuals.

What you need
Photocopiable pages 54 and 55.

What to do
As with the photograph album, photocopiable page 54 can be used in various ways. It can form part of a personal profile and/or be linked to topic work such as 'Ourselves' and 'People who help us', with the detail being filled in for real or imaginary people.

You can fill some or all of it in for younger children with the exception of the self-portrait which they can draw themselves, while older children can fill in the whole page by themselves.

Photocopiable page 55 can be used to make a cover for the passport, making a small booklet. Additional information could be added either on extra pages or on both sides of these two sheets, if your photocopier has a facility for copying both sides of a sheet of paper.

Wanted poster

Age range
Seven to eleven.

Group size
Individuals or small groups.

What you need
Photocopiable page 56.

What to do
Photocopiable page 56 can be used for keeping factual personal data on the children, or the children can fill it in with imaginary details of a make-believe character. It could also be a useful basis upon which the children can build information on a well-known personality or historical figure, or as an introduction page to a personal profile or portfolio.

The children can draw a 'portrait' in the blank square at the top of the page or stick in a photograph.

Telephone conversation

Age range
Eight to eleven.

Group size
Individuals or pairs.

What you need
Photocopiable page 57.

What to do
Photocopiable page 57 can be used by the children to practise direct speech skills which can be linked to any subject or topic. Both speech balloons can be filled in by the children, or to make work more specific you can complete part or all of one balloon and ask the children to fill in the rest. For example, you could fill in one balloon with questions and ask the children to write the replies in the other. Alternatively you could use the sheet for a cloze procedure activity.

   This is an effective way of testing children's knowledge and understanding of specific areas. It is also a good way of encouraging children to express any fears or problems which they may be encountering and can be used with photocopiable pages 19 to 21 in the 'Behaviour and rewards' chapter.

Opinion page

Age range
Six to eleven (with help from an adult for younger children).

Group size
Individuals.

What you need
Photocopiable page 58.

What to do
Photocopiable page 58 is a straightforward evaluation proforma which you can fill in with the children, or they can complete on their own. It can be used by the children to assess their own work, encouraging in them a sense of responsibility for their work, and thereby giving their comments and opinions significance and importance, as well as providing you with valuable evaluative diagnostic evidence. The sheet could be developed so that, if carefully and sensitively handled, children can evaluate and assess each other's work. You can also add your own prompts to make the proforma more specific to individual needs.

Letter writing sheet

Age range
Eight to eleven.

Group size
Individuals.

What you need
Photocopiable page 59.

What to do
Having to write for a specific purpose usually encourages children to produce their best efforts. Therefore, letter writing is often a good stimulus both for composition and for handwriting practice, and the scope for writing letters is almost limitless. The children could, for example, write letters to local councillors about a problem or an improvement that could be made in the local area; fan letters to their favourite television personalities; letters concerning topical issues to a politician; letters to their favourite authors saying why they like their books; letters to parents inviting them to a school function; thank you letters to a school visitor or to relatives.

Photocopiable page 59 provides a simple format for letter writing practice. The children could also design their own illustrations which could be placed over the original and then photocopied.

Reading diary and record, see page 31

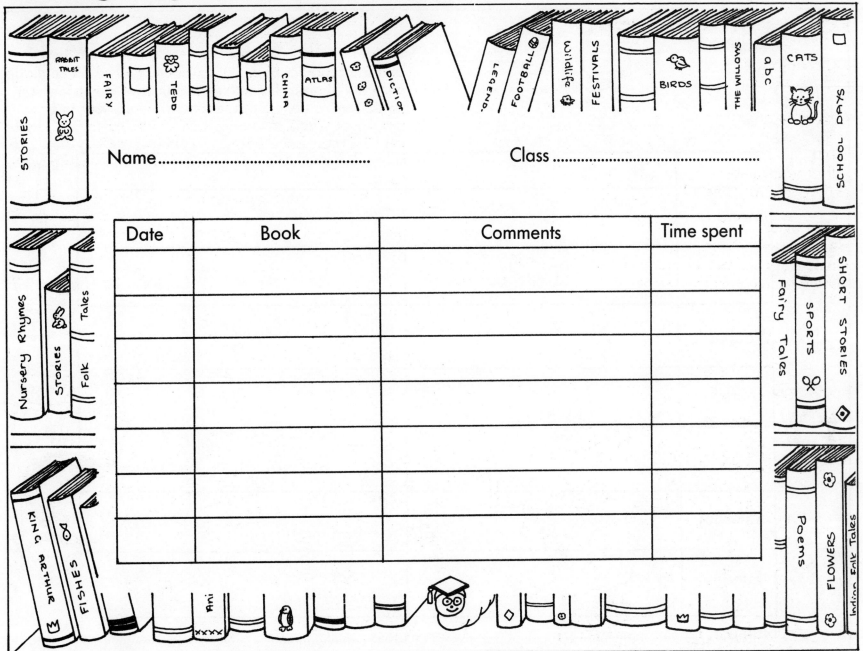

Name .... Class ....

Date	Book	Comments	Time spent

Reading diary and record, see page 31

Date:		
Monday		
Wednesday		
Thursday		
Friday		
Saturday		
Sunday		

Name ....   Class ....

Book reviews, see page 32

My book

My name ....

It was:

funny

sad

exciting

interesting

I liked...

Book reviews, see page 32

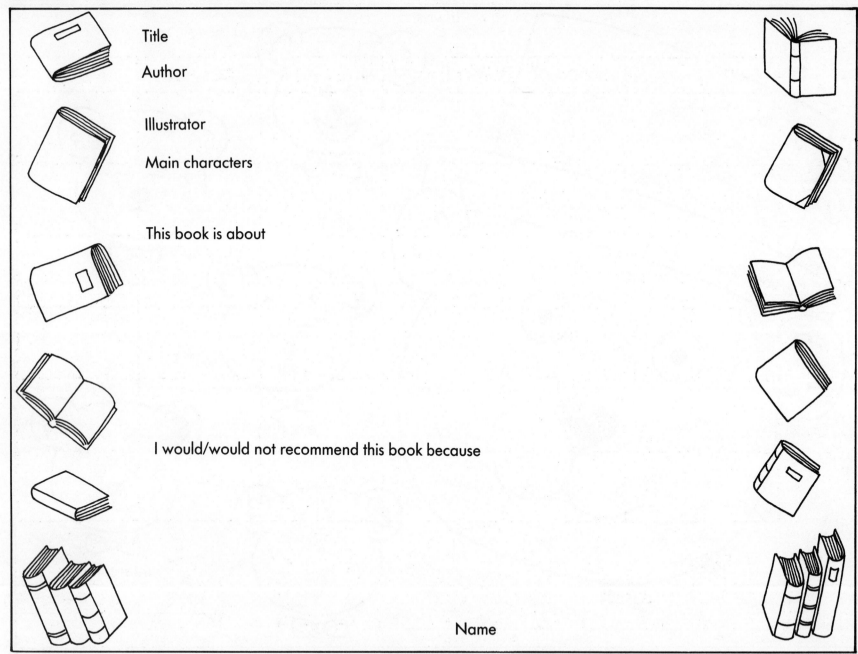

Title

Author

Illustrator

Main characters

This book is about

I would/would not recommend this book because

Name

Weather chart, see page 33

Week	Monday	Tuesday	Wednesday	Thursday	Friday
1					
2					
3					
4					
5					
6					

Growth chart, see page 33

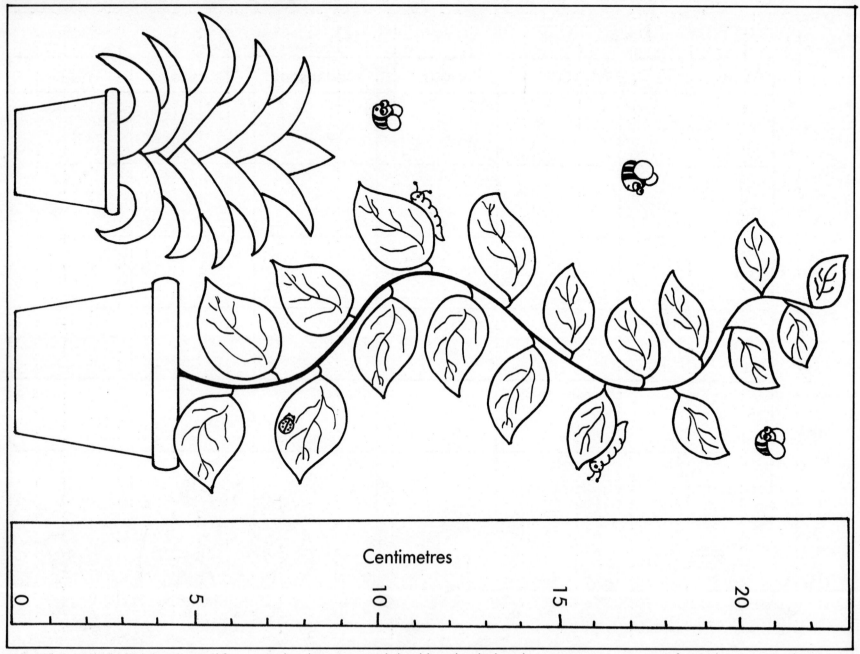

Centimetres

0   5   10   15   20

Blank grids and lined paper, see page 34

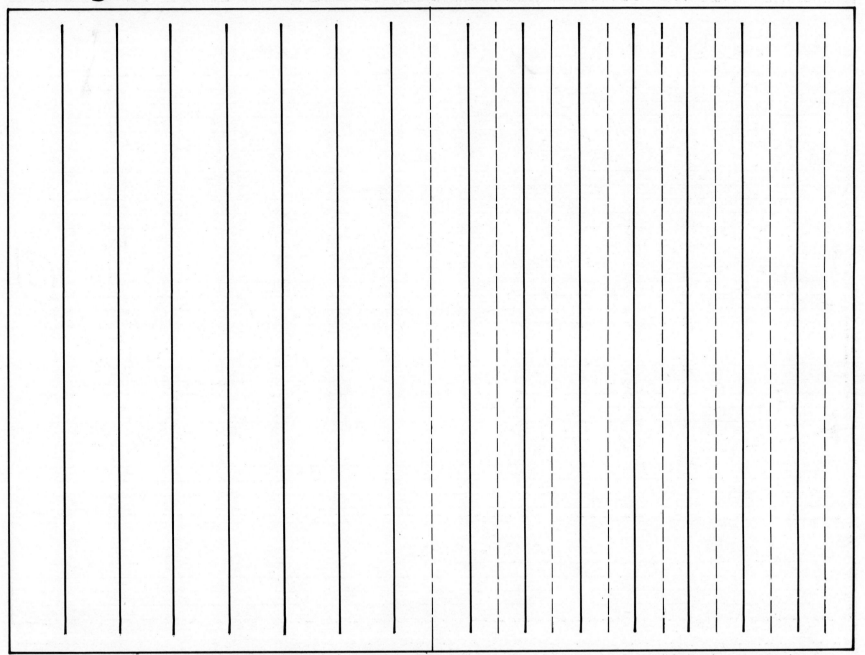

Blank grids and lined paper, see page 34

Blank grids and lined paper, see page 34

Map outlines, see page 34

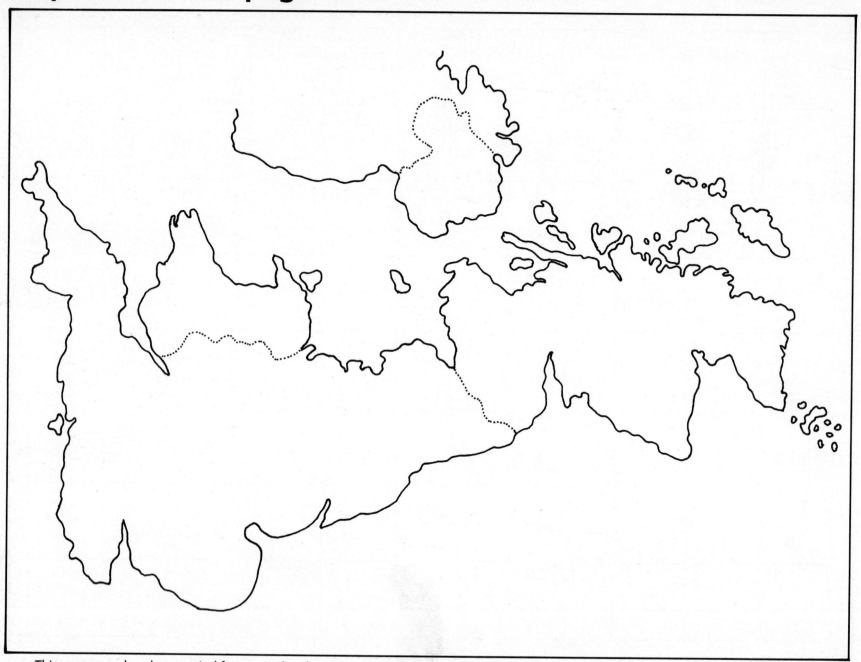

Map outlines, see page 34

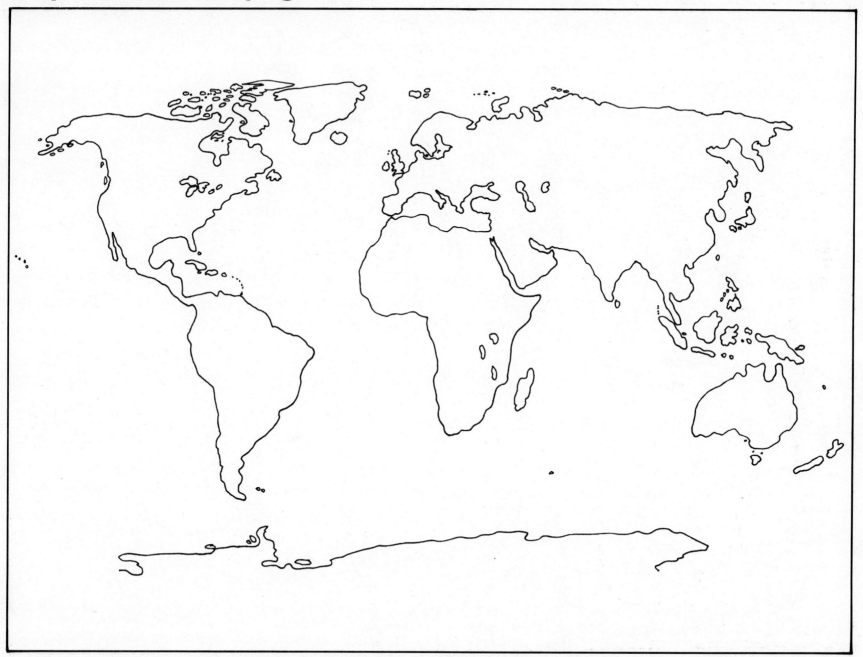

Map outlines, see page 34

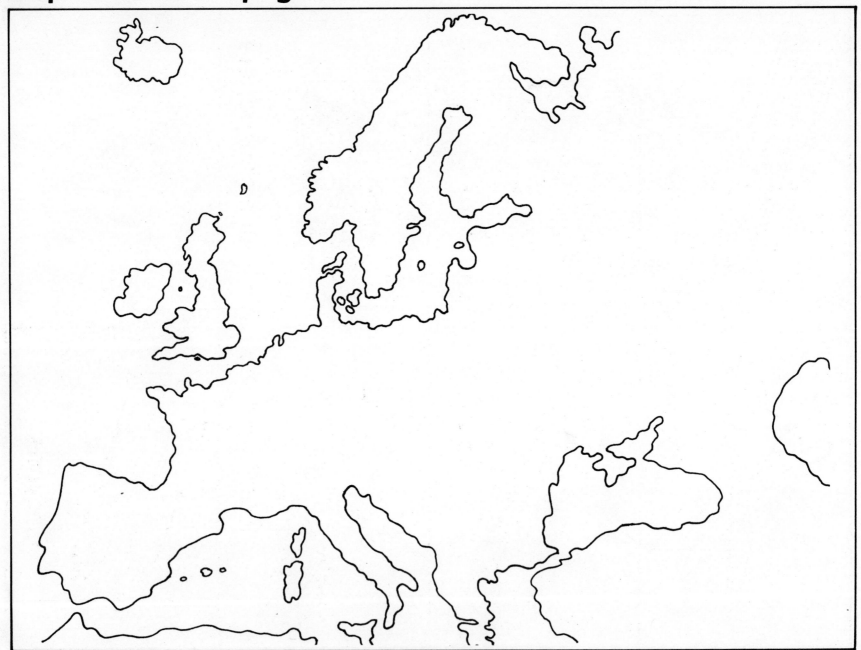

This page may be photocopied for use in the classroom and should not be declared in any return in respect of any photocopying licence.

Labels, see page 35

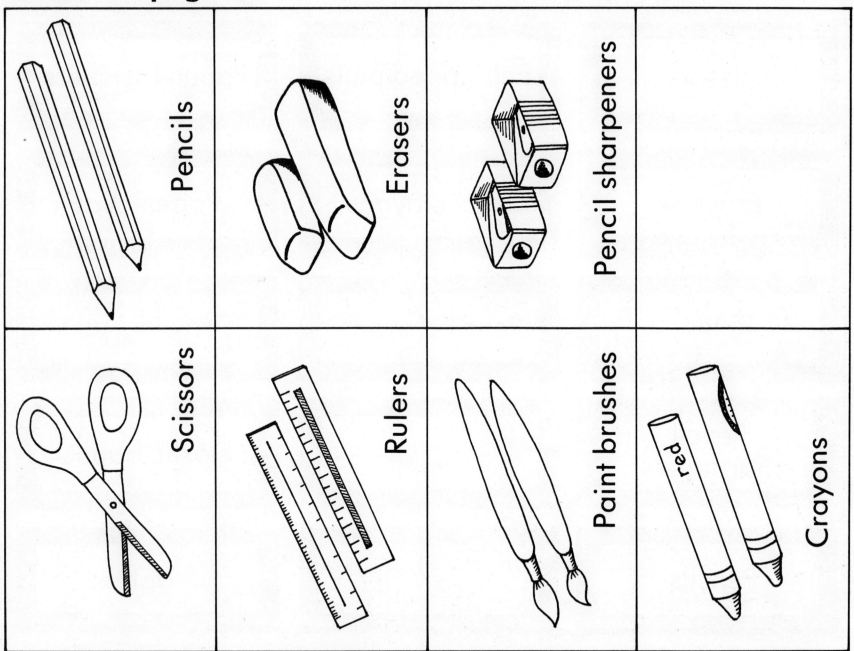

Pencils

Erasers

Pencil sharpeners

Scissors

Rulers

Paint brushes

red

Crayons

Labels, see page 35

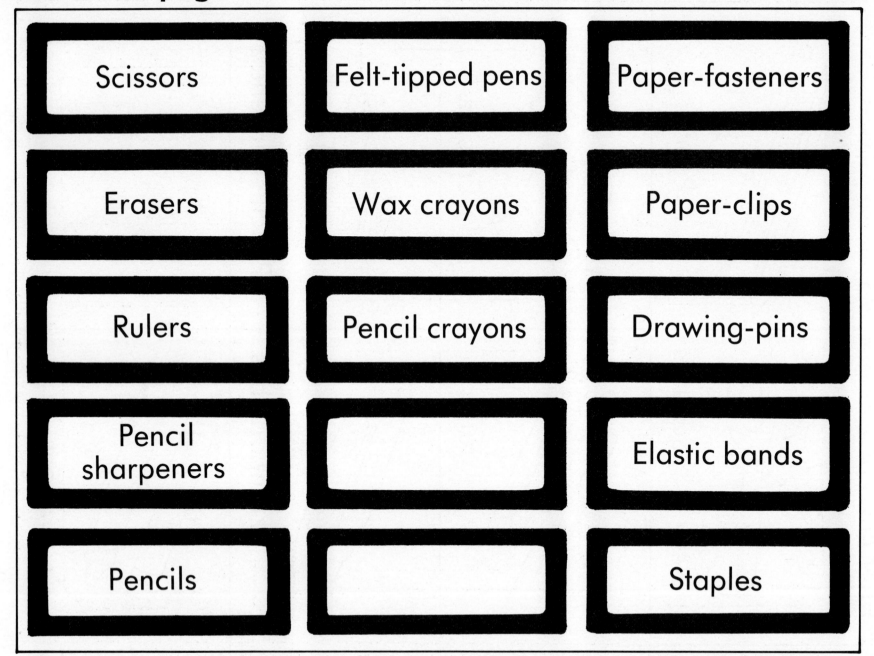

Scissors	Felt-tipped pens	Paper-fasteners
Erasers	Wax crayons	Paper-clips
Rulers	Pencil crayons	Drawing-pins
Pencil sharpeners		Elastic bands
Pencils		Staples

Photograph album, see page 35

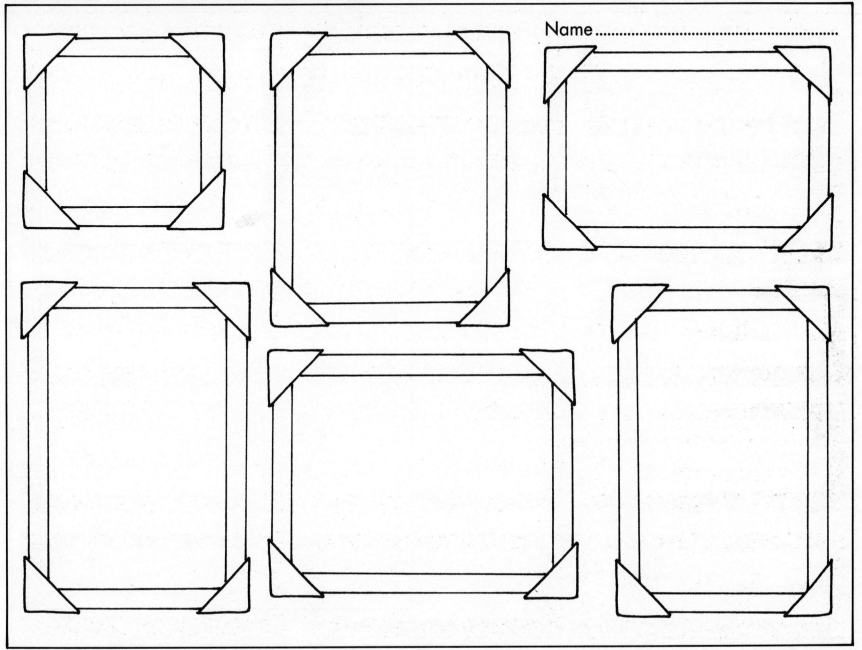

Name..

Passport, see page 36

Name

Age

Place of birth

Place of residence

Height   Weight

Colour of hair

Colour of eyes

Hobbies

Favourite book

Favourite food

Favourite colour

Favourite television programmes

At school I enjoy

People I admire

My ambitions

Passport, see page 36

DEPARTURE • **BIRMINGHAM** ✈

OTTAWA 6·6·91

9·9·91

SVERIGE ♔ ♔ ♔ 6·6·89

DOVER ARRIVAL 1·5·92

BAHAMAS

MOCKBÁ 30·6·89

21·6·90

DEPARTURE 5·4·91 **LONDON**

Passport

WANTED!

Dead or alive

Name _____

Age _____ years _____ months _____

_____

Colour of hair _____ Colour of eyes _____

Occupation _____
_____

Hobbies _____
_____

Likes _____
_____

Dislikes _____
_____
_____

Telephone conversation, see page 37

I thought the work was . .

Something I liked was . . .

I did not like . . .

I could do . . .

I learned to . . .

Subject .... Signed ....

Letter writing sheet, see page 38

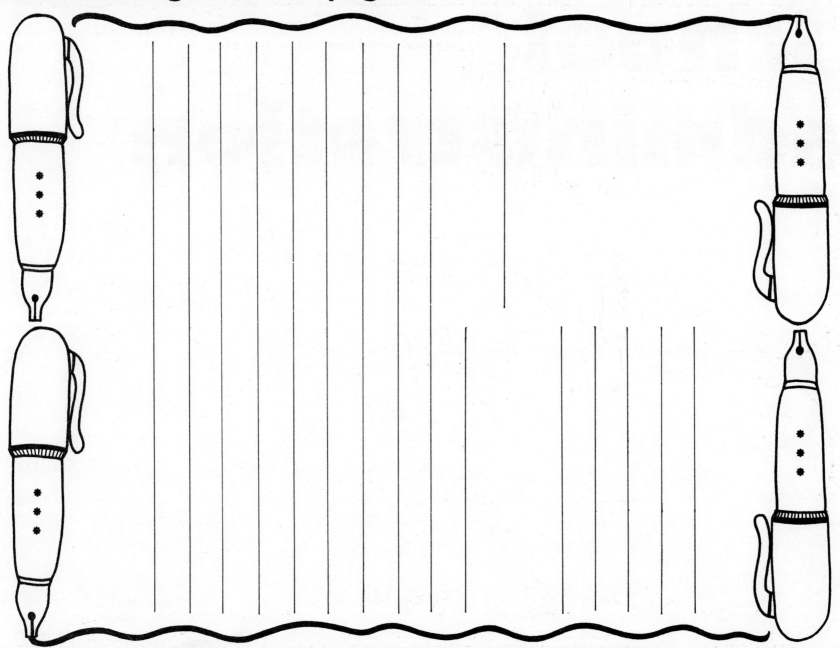

School administration

Staff noticeboard

What you need
Photocopiable pages 65, 66, 67, 68 and 69.

What to do
The staff noticeboard should be a focal point for teachers. A well-organised and attractive board helps make information accessible and prominent.

Labels: Page 65 provides labels to help organise the staff noticeboard. Cut out the labels, mount them on card and cover them with self-adhesive clear plastic. Then pin them to the noticeboard. There are also some blank labels which can be filled in as appropriate.

Diary: Keeping a diary of events on the staffroom noticeboard is most useful. Page 66 provides a basic chart which staff can fill in with their appointments, courses and other activities. Just as importantly, they must be encouraged to read the diary regularly so that everyone is kept up to date with all that is happening.

Timetable: The format on page 67 is suitable for most primary schools, but it can be adapted to suit individual needs by, for example, adding additional lines or blanking out the afternoon break.

Rotas: Photocopiable page 68 is self-explanatory and is flexible enough to be used for a number of purposes, including playground and assembly rotas. There is room at the top of the sheet to say what each rota is for.

Useful telephone numbers: Page 69 should include the most frequently used telephone numbers, such as those of the LEA offices and supply staff. This way numbers are immediately to hand, and it saves looking for those often elusive phone books!

Supply staff

What you need
Photocopiable page 70 and information as listed below.

What to do
At one time or another all schools have to call upon the services of a supply teacher, on either a long- or a short-term basis. Often when they arrive there is not enough time to explain to them fully all of the school's routines. It is therefore a good idea to keep an up-to-date file specifically for these teachers, containing information and details of all relevant school procedures. This should be set out in a succinct, friendly and welcoming way.

Photocopiable page 70 provides an introductory sheet for such a file. The first half of the sheet provides space to list all the staff in the school and their specific areas of responsibility, and the other half is for any other relevant general information. Other information provided may include some of the following:
- a plan of the school and a map of the local area;
- school times;
- rotas and timetables;
- fire drill procedure;
- playtime routines;
- coffee and tea-making facilities and charges;
- copies of relevant school policies such as basic aims and objectives;
- tuck shop arrangements.

These folders can also prove useful for new permanent members of staff.

Course evaluation sheet

What you need
Photocopiable page 71.

What to do
With so many demands upon teachers' time, it is often difficult to find time to report back adequately on various courses attended. The form on photocopiable page 71 is intended to help alleviate this problem by providing a structured format which is easy to fill in. It should be completed succinctly by anyone who has attended a course, giving relevant information and a course rating, for example, from one for poor to five for excellent.

The completed sheets should be kept centrally so that they are easily accessible to other staff who may want to read them. Staff will then easily be able to gain further details, if they wish, from the course attenders personally. All this means that the process of deciding whether or not to attend a particular course is carried out on a more informed and accurate basis rather than wasting time on research. It also helps avoid the risk of attending inappropriate courses.

Assembly record

Date	Theme	Details
30·10·91	Harvest Festival - Class Y6. (Mr. Jones).	Hymns + readings. Guests invited inc. Vicar and local elderly. Lovely display.
31·10·91	Harvests around the world. (Mrs. Davies).	Looking at the different seasons + harvests in parts of Africa and Asia.
1·11·91	Class assembly -Y3: Patterns. (Miss. Cameron).	Children talked about Roman mosaics, the importance of patterns in Islam, various religious symbols, materials etc.
4·11·91	Visit from Mr. Singh.	Showed children various Sikh artefacts, explained about worship in the Gurudwara. (Class Y5 going to visit next week)

Assembly record

What you need
Photocopiable page 72.

What to do
Photocopiable page 72 is intended to be used as a means of keeping brief records concerning each act of collective worship within school. As each sheet is completed it can be filed and kept centrally. This record is useful when planning future acts of worship to ensure that a balance is kept as required by the 1988 Education Reform Act and to avoid repetition. The record can also be examined by any interested parties wishing to see what form the school's acts of worship are taking.

Accident and sick notes

What you need
Photocopiable page 73.

What to do
Most schools send notes home when a child has an accident at school, particularly if it involves a head injury. Often it is also helpful to provide a note for parents if a child has been unwell. The 'accident' letter and 'sick note' on photocopiable page 73 are easily completed. They are a little unusual in that they are illustrated, but more visually attractive letters seem to have a greater chance of being read. This is particularly important for letters concerning children's health.

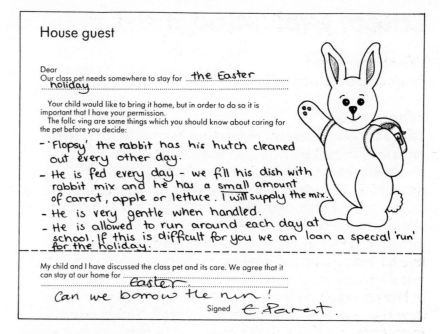

House guest

Dear
Our class pet needs somewhere to stay for ...the Easter
holiday...

Your child would like to bring it home, but in order to do so it is important that I have your permission.
The follcving are some things which you should know about caring for the pet before you decide:

- 'Flopsy' the rabbit has his hutch cleaned out every other day.
- He is fed every day - we fill his dish with rabbit mix and he has a small amount of carrot, apple or lettuce. I will supply the mix.
- He is very gentle when handled.
- He is allowed to run around each day at school. If this is difficult for you we can loan a special 'run' for the holiday.

My child and I have discussed the class pet and its care. We agree that it can stay at our home for ....
......................Easter......................
Can we borrow the run!
Signed E. Parent.

Houseguest

What you need
Photocopiable page 74.

What to do
Many classes have small animals as classroom pets and they are usually very educational, interesting and often highly entertaining. However, caring for the pet during weekends and holidays can often prove to be difficult. The photocopiable letter on page 74 can be sent to parents of children who are keen to care for the 'pet houseguest' and has space for vital care details to be noted down.

School trips

What you need
Photocopiable pages 75 and 76.

What to do
The letter on photocopiable page 75 is a fairly flexible letter which can be adapted to fit most organised trips. There is included in the letter a permission slip for parents to sign and return to school.

Photocopiable page 76 is a school trip record sheet which can be used as a simple way of collating information when organising a trip. You can use it to keep a record of the number of children going on the trip and how much money has been collected. Finally, it can be used as a check list on the day. It may be useful to provide the head or school secretary with a copy of the completed form so that they are able to answer queries or make contact on the day of the trip.

It is important to give any helpers full information and ensure that adults who are responsible for groups of children have complete lists of their charges, the timings, destinations and so forth.

School certificates

What you need
Photocopiable page 77.

What to do
Children like to receive certificates, and the two provided on photocopiable page 77 should prove to be very useful. The attendance award certificate is a positive way to encourage good attendance. Children who have a good attendance record and are awarded a certificate are usually encouraged to continue in this way.

The 'goodbye and good luck' certificate can be used in a number of ways. It could be presented to pupils who are leaving, particularly those moving up to the next phase in their education, for example, moving from infant to junior school. In this case the certificate could be enlarged and signed by all the staff, duplicated and given to each child. If only one child is leaving, it could be signed by all the children in his class. The certificate could even be used for a colleague!

Staff noticeboard, see page 61

Rotas	Timetables	Union
Courses	Newsflash	Diary
Staff notice	General information	

Staff noticeboard, see page 61

Week beginning ....

	Morning	Afternoon
Monday		
Tuesday		
Wednesday		
Thursday		
Friday		

Staff noticeboard, see page 61

Timetable

			Break			Lunch			Break	
Monday										
Tuesday										
Wednesday										
Thursday										
Friday										

Staff noticeboard, see page 61

Rota for..

Week beginning	Monday	Tuesday	Wednesday	Thursday	Friday

Staff noticeboard, see page 61

Useful telephone numbers

Supply staff

L E A numbers

Governors

Outside agencies

This page may be photocopied for use in the classroom and should not be declared in any return in respect of any photocopying licence.

Welcome to our school

Deputy:

Headteacher:

Staff:

- -

General information

The attendance registers are kept:

They are sent to every

The classroom keys are kept:

The procedure for getting stock is:

First Aid for the children is administered by:

and it is kept in

Course evaluation sheet, see page 62

Title	Date

Venue

Resumé of information gained:

General comments:

Usefulness/interest score; 1 2 3 4 5 +

               (poor)→(excellent)

Signed

Assembly record sheet, see page 62

Assembly record

Date	Theme	Details

Acciden

Dear

Your child _ _ _ _ _ _ _ _ _ _ _ _ had an

accident in school today.

S/he _ _ _ _ _ _ _ _ _ _ _ _ _ _ _ _ _ _

If you are at all concerned about your child's injury please see your doctor.

Yours sincerely,

Class teacher

Head teacher

Just a note

Dear

Your child   was unwell

at school today. S/he   complained of

_ _
_ _

Yours sincerely,

Class teacher

Head teacher

Houseguest

Dear
Our class pet needs somewhere to stay for ....
....

    Your child would like to bring it home, but in order to do so it is important that I have your permission.
    The following are some things which you should know about caring for the pet before you decide:

- -

My child and I have discussed the class pet and its care. We agree that it can stay at our home for ....
....

Signed

School outing

Dear parents

We are organising an outing to ....
.... on ....
we will leave at ....
and return by ....
    The cost per child is ....
    Under the terms of the Education Reform Act this is a voluntary contribution, but if the costs are not met the trip may, unfortunately, have to be cancelled. If you wish to enquire about payments, please do not hesitate in coming to see us.
    The children will need ....
    If you are willing for your child to take part in this outing please sign and return the permission slip below by ....

Yours sincerely

Class teacher

- -

I give permission for my child ....
To go on the school trip to ....
I understand that reasonable care and vigilance will be exercised by the teacher and it is on this basis that I give my consent for my child to attend.

Signed

School trips, see page 64

Name	Permission slip	Payments					Total

This page may be photocopied for use in the classroom and should not be declared in any return in respect of any photocopying licence.

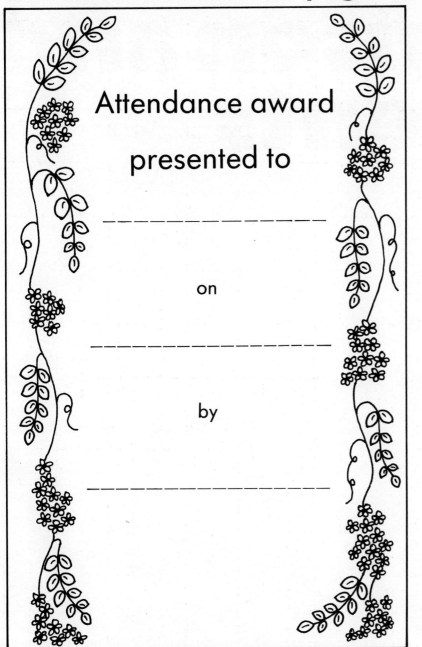

Attendance award

presented to

_____

on

_____

by

_____

Goodbye

and

good luck

from

Parent liaison and school events

School events

What you need
Photocopiable page 85.

What to do
Photocopiable page 85 provides various designs to use when holding popular school events. They can be used as letter headings or to make small posters. Most schools have open days, sports days, leavers' assemblies and parent consultations, and all the headings can make very effective invitations for parents.

There are also various certificates throughout the book which would be appropriate to present to children on occasions such as sports days and leavers' assemblies (see pages 27 and 28).

Fund raising

What you need
Photocopiable pages 86 and 87.

What to do
Fund-raising events have become part of every school's calendar. There is a multitude of ways to raise funds and photocopiable page 86 provides some designed headings which can be used for letters, handbills and small posters to advertise a summer fair, car boot sale, barn dance and disco.

Photocopiable page 87 provides a layout for a sponsorship form which can be used or adapted to suit most events. Space has been provided for the insertion of sponsorship details and authorisation.

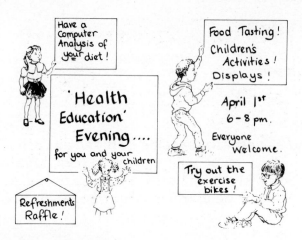

Curriculum evenings

What you need
Photocopiable page 88.

What to do
To keep parents informed of the latest initiatives and directives on curriculum matters, it is often a good idea to organise 'curriculum evenings' where specific areas of the curriculum are chosen and activities arranged around them.

In order to get a good attendance on these occasions, it is better to organise practical activities rather than just a talk. Picking a more 'fun' title than just 'Maths' or 'Science' can also encourage the less enthusiastic to attend. If the evening can be organised as a family event, rather than involving just parents, the attendance will also probably be greater.

Photocopiable page 88 provides a format for a small poster or handbill for such an event. The large square is intended for the main title of the evening while the smaller boxes can be used to highlight certain activities, such as raffles and competitions.

Book week

Age range
Whole school.

What you need
Photocopiable page 89.

What to do
Book weeks are a popular way of heightening children's awareness and enjoyment of books. There are numerous activities that can be held during a book week including inviting local librarians, authors and poets (amateur or professional), dressing up as characters from favourite books and holding competitions and quizzes. All these activities provide a great opportunity to involve parents and the local community.

Photocopiable page 89 shows two designs that can be used for letterheads or handbills, and two presentation labels. Parents can be encouraged to buy a book for the school from a recommended list of reasonably priced books, or to donate some money towards buying a book. The labels can then be stuck into the front of these books as a way of expressing thanks. There is space on each presentation label to write who donated the book, the date and the school's name.

School noticeboard

What you need
Photocopiable page 90.

What to do
A community noticeboard is an effective way to keep parents informed of what is going on in school and helps to improve communication and liaison between parents and school. There is plenty of information which would be usefully displayed on such a board, for example, forthcoming school and community events, useful addresses and telephone numbers, names of members of staff, copies of the latest letters sent home to parents, a map of the area and a plan of the school.

The labels provided on photocopiable page 90 serve as a useful means of organising such a noticeboard. They can be covered with self-adhesive plastic to keep them in good condition.

Bulletins and newsletters

What you need
Photocopiable page 91.

What to do
One easy way of ensuring good communication between parents and school is to provide parents with regular letters telling them of future events to be held at school. Make the letters eyecatching to help ensure that they are actually read, and if you let the children colour the line illustrations, it heightens the chances of the letters actually getting home!

The bulletins can take many forms, for example, a newspaper page or a handbill, and varying the format helps to maintain interest. Keeping parents aware of school events promotes the idea of partnership and co-operation in their child's education.

Photocopiable page 91 provides two headings and designs which should prove useful when compiling bulletins; the children could also provide extra drawings.

Parent handbook

What you need
Photocopiable pages 91 and 92.

What to do
In addition to the school prospectus, it is often helpful to have another booklet or pamphlet aimed at parents whose children are new to the school, especially those with children starting their first year of schooling.

Useful information that could be provided in such a handbook includes:
- tips on helping children's education at home before and during their school years, for example, reading, listening and practical activities;
- school routines and rules;
- the basic aims and philosophy of the school and its presentation of the curriculum;
- schemes used by the school, letter formation and home reading initiatives;
- community information.

Photocopiable page 91 provides a heading and a large illustration which could be used as the front cover. The other adult and child pictures on this page could be used as illustrations, inside the handbook.

Photocopiable page 92 is intended to be a sheet that can be included in the front of the parent handbook. It should be completed by the child and parent after the child has attended school for some weeks. With pages that include a parent and child input, community information, relevant school details and space left for data on school milestones, it can be hoped that the handbook will be kept for a good period of time.

Parent helpers

What you need
Photocopiable pages 93 and 94.

What to do
Asking parents to help in school has many advantages – you gain extra pairs of hands in the classroom while parents gain a sense of involvement and proof that the school values them.

Many mums and dads, though, are rather nervous of coming into school or feel that they have nothing to offer. To overcome this, send out a friendly questionnaire asking parents what commitments they could make and in what areas they feel they could help. Photocopiable page 93 provides a parent helper questionnaire which should be appropriate for most schools and parents. However, space has been left to enable you to add your own questions if needed.

In addition to the questionnaire, photocopiable page 94 provides a letter inviting parents to come into school, and also a thank-you letter for parents who actually do come and help.

You may feel the need to add a footnote to the invitation letter explaining that parents may not be working with their own children and that teachers will not be available for consultation on their child's progress during these times!

Parent checklist

What you need
Photocopiable page 95.

What to do
Photocopiable page 95 is intended to be used as a prompt sheet for parents whose children have just started school. It tries to include all the questions that parents frequently ask, and leaves space for you to add any others. Many of the answers will probably already be found in the literature that the school gives to parents, such as the prospectus, but often verbal answers and reassurances are needed. This prompt sheet could be included in the material given to new parents either with the appropriate answers or purely as questions that can be asked at initial parent/teacher meetings. It should not only be a useful aid to them, but also show the school's wish to fully inform its parents.

Healthy eating

Age range
Children aged eight to eleven or parents.

What you need
Photocopiable page 96.

What to do
Photocopiable page 96 is a simple advice sheet on 'healthy' food which can be used as guidance for parents as to what to include in their children's packed lunches. It could be sent to parents or studied by children as part of a 'healthy eating' campaign, or included as a page in the school handbook.

Road safety

Age range
Parents and children.

What you need
Photocopiable page 97.

What to do
Unfortunately there are very few schools which have not had any of their children involved in a road accident. Most schools do their utmost to instill road safety skills in their children, but children follow by example and if they see familiar adults taking risks on the roads, they will assume that this is the norm.

Photocopiable page 97 is a straightforward sheet, aimed at parents, which explains the basics of road safety. It could be used as a handout for parents whose children are new to the school, as a page in the school's handbook or as part of a campaign on improving children's safety skills. It is probably most effectively used in conjunction with other literature and practical activities on road safety.

Open day

Sports day

Leavers assembly

GOOD LUCK

Summer fair

Car boot sale

Disco

Barn dance

Fund raising, see page 79

Sponsorship form for ....

Name ....

Signed ....

Class...............

Curriculum evenings, see page 80

Book week, see page 80

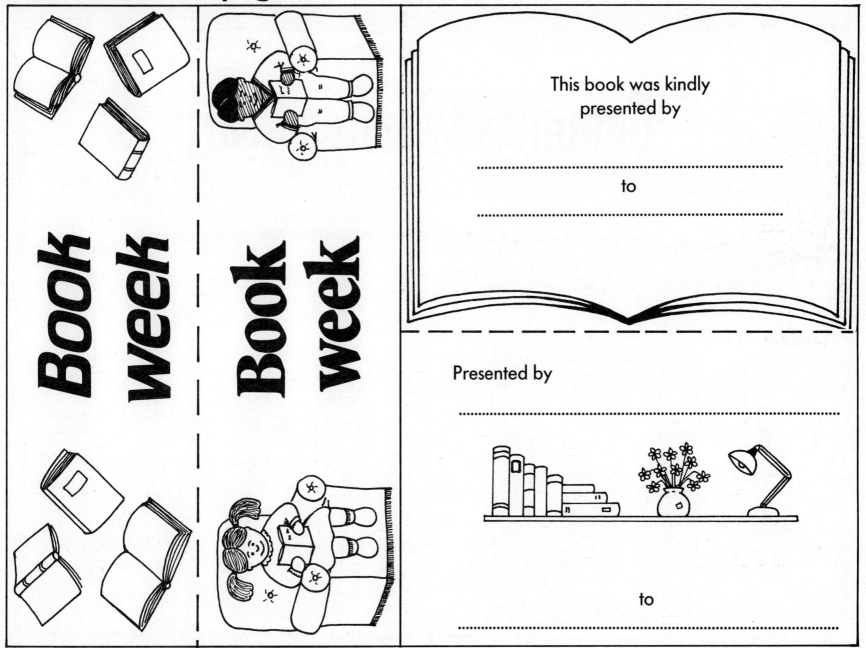

Book week

Book week

This book was kindly
presented by

....

to

....

Presented by

....

to

....

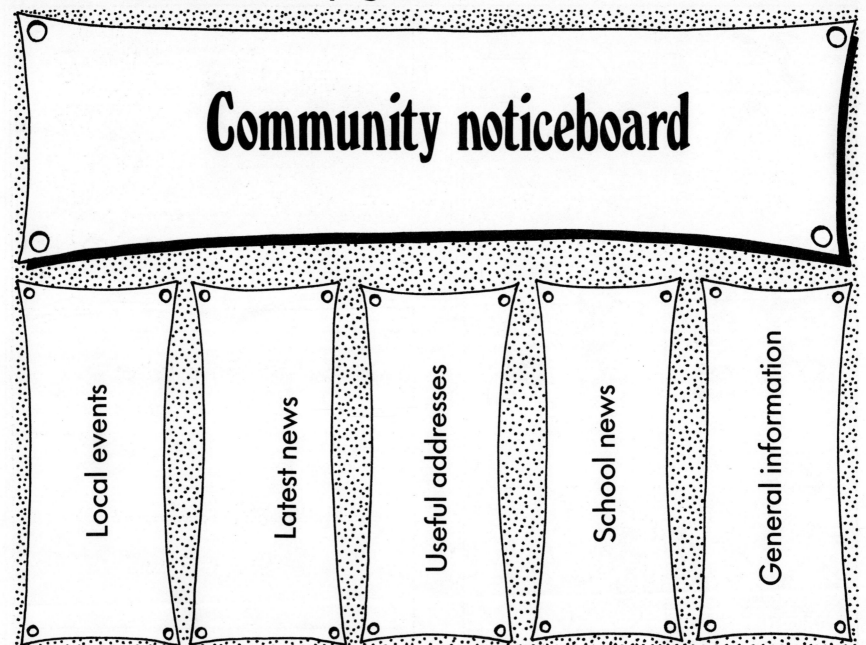

Community noticeboard

Local events

Latest news

Useful addresses

School news

General information

Bulletins and newsletters and parent handbook, see pages 81 and 82

School newsletter

PARENT

HANDBOOK

SCHOOL

BULLETIN

This page may be photocopied for use in the classroom and should not be declared in any return in respect of any photocopying licence.

All about me . . .

I can write my name

....

I look like this

I am in class

....

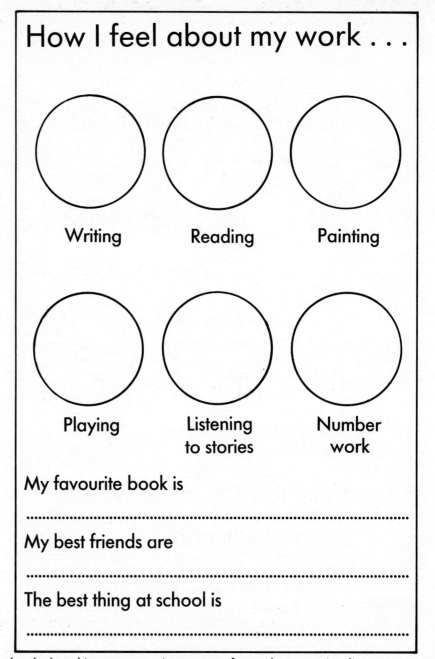

How I feel about my work . . .

Writing   Reading   Painting

Playing   Listening to stories   Number work

My favourite book is

....

My best friends are

....

The best thing at school is

....

Parent helpers, see page 83

Dear Parent/Guardian,
Please complete the questionnaire below. This will then enable us to organise the time you can spare us in school to the benefit of both the children and yourself.

Yours sincerely

Headteacher

Class teacher

- -

Name
I am available on:
Monday   Tuesday   Wednesday   Thursday   Friday

For approximately:
1 hour   1 morning   1 afternoon   occasionally   other (specify)

I would prefer to help:
individuals   small groups   outside of classes

I am interested in
- helping with art/craft/design work;
- sharing books with the children eg reading together;
- helping in the library;
- cooking activities;
- general classroom activities;
- other (please specify)

Thank you for your co-operation, we look forward to seeing you soon.

Dear Parent/Guardian,
Could you spare us some of your time? We welcome help from parents in our classrooms and around the school. Even if you feel you have nothing you can offer, we are sure you can help us in some way. Maybe you have a hobby you could share, a practical skill or are a good listener – the children will love to talk to you!

We can find activities to suit you – not only will it give our children the benefit of relating to other adults, but you will probably find you will enjoy yourself and get to know the school even better.

If you are interested and think you could give us some time, either come in and see us or fill in the slip below. We will give you a short questionnaire to complete which simply asks you about the time you are able to spare and the help you are interested in giving.

Your sincerely

Headteacher

Class teacher

I am interested in helping in school. I will contact the school/Please send me more information. (Delete as appropriate.)

Signed

Thank you

For all your help . . .
Presented to

....

from
all the staff and children

Parent checklist, see page 83

Twenty questions you may wish to ask . . .

1. Has my child had a pre-school jab?

2. When does my child have routine health checks at school?

3. What is the routine if my child needs to take medicine at school?

4. What happens if my child has an accident?

5. Do the children stay in the same class each year or are the classes reorganised?

6. What is the procedure for school outings?

7. Is there a school uniform or school colours?

8. Should my child have special clothes for PE?

9. Is there any formal system for collecting school funds?

10. What are the dinner options open to my child?

11. What is the system for school dinners and sandwiches?

12. Can my child bring drinks and snacks for playtime?

13. What is the procedure for my child to bring reading books home?

14. Can I attend any school assemblies?

15. What form do assemblies and RE lessons take?

16. Is there any way I can help the school?

17. What do I do if I wish to see the head or class teacher?

18. What opportunities are there for meeting with the parent-governors?

19.

20.

This page may be photocopied for use in the classroom and should not be declared in any return in respect of any photocopying licence.

Healthy eating

School packed lunch and snack ideas

Sandwiches and rolls — choose wholemeal bread and nutritious fillings like:

tomato and low-fat cheese

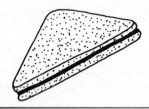
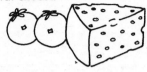

peanut butter

tuna and salad

Afters — avoid sugary foods and try:

yoghurt

fresh fruit

Drinks — choose fruit juice or milk rather than squash.

Snacks — have fresh vegetable or fruit pieces.

Try to avoid or have as occasional treats: Sugary food like sweets and chocolate   Salty and fried foods like crisps

Crossing the road

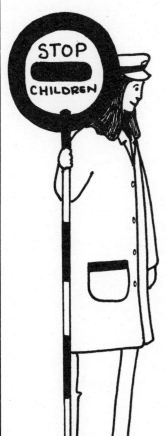

Always try to use a Zebra or Pelican crossing.

When you are near to school always cross with the School Crossing Patrol ('Lollipop' person).

If there is not one of the above then:
- Find a safe place to cross the road (not by parked cars if possible);
- Stand towards the kerb of the pavement and look all around and listen for any traffic;
- If there is some traffic by you let it pass and look all around again;
- When there is no traffic walk across the road, but keep looking and listening, until you are safely across.

Wear something light or reflective, especially in the dark.

Useful road signs:

Children going to or from school

Pedestrian crossing ahead

No pedestrians

Special occasions

Birthdays

Age range
Four to eleven.

Group size
Any.

What you need
Photocopiable page 114 or 115.

What to do
Children's birthdays can be celebrated in a number of ways. For example, you can hold special assemblies with imitation cakes with the appropriate number of candles lit; birthday noticeboards with the children's names displayed each week or calendar month; classroom events, and so on.

Birthdays can be used as an early means of data collection and pictorial representation. Photocopiable page 114 shows a chart specifically designed to record class birthdays. The spaces could be coloured to the appropriate level, or pictures such as faces or cakes could be drawn or stuck on as needed. The collecting of data can be done by individuals or groups, with or without teacher help. Enlarge the graph sheet to A3 size, if possible. Photocopiable page 115 shows a number of birthday designs that can be used on cards and worksheets, or as headings for stories, poems and number work. There is also a birthday certificate that can be presented to pupils.

The children could make up a birthday honours list by discovering which famous people have a birthday on the same day as themselves. Children could research into the year they were born and find out about the major events of that year. They could also look at star signs and their supposed characteristics or see what their symbol is from the Chinese Calendar (see Chinese New Year on page 128).

World Children's Day

Age range
Six to eleven.

Group size
Individuals or groups.

What you need
Photocopiable page 116 and possibly further information about this celebration.

What to do
World Children's Day is celebrated on 15 June. This day was initiated by the United Nations with the intention of making the world think about its children. Therefore it is a day when children can be encouraged to think about other children who are less fortunate than themselves, for example, those who are caught up in wars, who are victims of famine and drought, who live with excessive pollution or whose homelands are being destroyed.

Many organisations, such as Save the Children Fund, Action Aid, CARE, OXFAM and Third World First, are happy to supply information about these issues.

Photocopiable page 116 can be used as a heading for a 'Children's Charter'. This can be drawn up by the children themselves, who should decide upon what they think are children's rights. They could also look at the different lifestyles of children around the world and compare them to their own through art work, descriptive writing and role-play. The illustrations could be used to make a greetings card, booklet or as a centre piece for a 'World's Children' mobile.

United Nations Day

Age range
Six to eleven.

Group size
Individuals or whole class.

What you need
Photocopiable page 116 and additional information, if needed.

What to do
The United Nations was established on 24 October 1945. It is an international body with headquarters in New York. Its aims are to maintain peace and global security, ensure human rights and promote co-operation between nations and so tackle economic, cultural, environmental and social issues.

The United Nations' administrative work is dealt with by the secretariat, of which the Secretary General is the head. The General Assembly involves delegates from all the member countries, and they discuss the many issues which arise. The Security Council has five permanent members (UK, USSR, USA, France and China) and ten non-permanent members, and it is they who make the final policy decisions.

The United Nations also funds many other organisations, such as the World Health Organisation (WHO) and United Nations Educational, Scientific and Cultural Organisation (UNESCO).

United Nations Day on 24 October provides an opportunity to discuss with the children this important international body and its role. The United Nations does not always enjoy total success, but its existence is a necessity. This can be discussed with older children, as well as questions such as – why is the United Nations sometimes divided? Can the United Nations enforce its decisions? What would the children do and say if they were in the United Nations?

Photocopiable page 116 can be used to make greetings cards, handbills to advertise a special assembly, or as a heading for written work. Younger children can be involved in this work too, and although they will not understand much of the work that the United Nations does, they should be able to grasp the ideas of co-operation, friendship and harmony.

Commonwealth Day

Age range
Seven to eleven.

Group size
Any.

What you need
Photocopiable page 117.

What to do
As with other 'international' days, Commonwealth Day on 11 March can provide an opportunity for children to look at different ways of life and the idea of co-operation between different people and nations.

The British Commonwealth includes Australia, Canada, New Zealand, Jamaica, India and many other African, Asian and Caribbean states. It is a free association of states who were once members of the British Empire, although not all countries with this history are members of the Commonwealth, for example, Pakistan. The Commonwealth has no real power, but can be a useful means for heads of state from different parts of the world to meet. It organises educational exchanges and enables various countries to organise cultural and personal links. It is a multi-nation, multi-race and multi-faith organisation.

The design on photocopiable page 117 shows the flags of a number of Commonwealth countries. It could be used as a heading to children's written work or in a display on the Commonwealth. The children could also try to find out to which countries the various flags belong. Flags make an interesting topic and their histories are often fascinating. Children could design their own flags and logos for various things, including the Commonwealth.

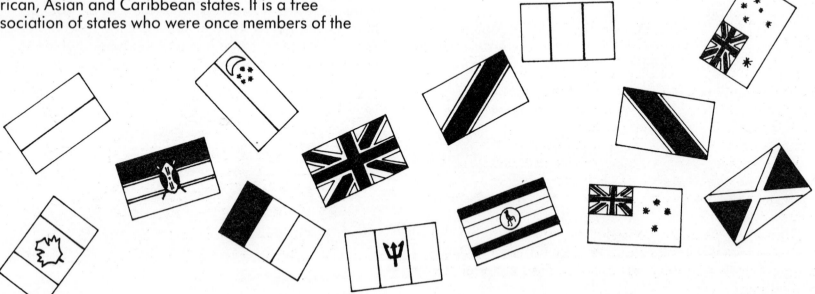

Remembrance Sunday

Age range
A matter for individual judgement.

Group size
Individuals or groups.

What you need
Photocopiable page 117.

What to do
Remembrance Sunday is the day when the people who died in both World Wars are remembered. It usually falls on the Sunday nearest to 11 November, which was Armistice Day at the end of the First World War.

As well as taking part by selling poppies, you could also have special assemblies or lessons explaining the reasons behind this day.

The Cenotaph, in London, which is illustrated on photocopiable page 117, is central to the events of Remembrance Sunday in Britain and on this day wreaths are laid there by the Queen and various dignitaries. It is a plain white memorial to the fallen of the First and Second World Wars. The word Cenotaph is derived from Greek and means 'empty tomb'.

Photocopiable page 117 could be used to illustrate children's written work about war, the reasons behind this day, their feelings on conflicts, how they would act as a head of state or ambassador to the United Nations and so on.

Grandparents and other members of the local community who lived through the Second World War could be invited by the class to tell of their experiences and feelings.

New Year

Age range
Six to eleven.

Group size
Individuals or groups.

What you need
Photocopiable page 118.

What to do
Photocopiable page 118 shows a design for New Year with a Scottish theme. Hogmanay, as New Year is called in Scotland, is often celebrated there to a greater extent than Christmas. The design on photocopiable page 118 can be used to make greetings cards or as a heading for New Year's resolutions.

The dove of peace, on the same page, can also be used at this time of the year with messages of good fortune and peace in the coming year. Children could note down or draw what they hope to achieve in the coming year. Older children can widen their thoughts to take account of the world situation or local issues, such as environmental problems.

All Fools' Day

Age range
Five to eleven.

Group size
Individuals, groups or whole class.

What you need
Photocopiable page 119.

What to do
All Fools' Day or April Fools' Day can be great fun for children if they are permitted to play practical jokes and tricks. However, boundaries do need to be set so that school life is not disrupted too much.

Page 119 can be used for other activities based on this day. The design can be used as a heading for children's written work, funny stories or poems.

Saint Valentine's Day

Age range
Six to eleven.

Group size
Individuals.

What you need
Photocopiable page 119.

What to do
The origins of this festival are varied. It was fabled that 14 February was the day on which birds chose their mates. Also, the Romans used to hold a festival of love called Lupercalia on or near this day. St Valentine is thought to have been put to death by the Romans for his Christian beliefs, and his execution was carried out about the same time as the Roman festival, which may have led to his association with love.

    The design on photocopiable page 119 is intended to be used by the children for making Valentine cards. Alternatively, the hearts could be copied, coloured and cut out to make mobiles. It could also be used as a heading for written work, for example, who do the pupils see as having real 'heart', perhaps those who help others?

Mothering Sunday

Age range
Five to eleven.

Group size
Individuals or small groups.

What you need
Photocopiable page 120.

What to do
Mothering Sunday always falls on the fourth Sunday in Lent and is linked to the Christian church. In the past on Mothering Sunday people would visit their churches and families. Nowadays people tend to call this celebration 'Mother's Day' and celebrate it by sending cards and presents to their mothers.

    The two illustrations on photocopiable page 120 are intended to be used by the children to make greetings cards or as illustrations for a piece of writing, for example, a poem describing mum, a list of all the things mums do for their children, famous mums of the past and present, mums around the world and the problems they face.

    Obviously, sensitivity must be shown to those children whose mothers are no longer with them, and acceptable alternatives can usually be found.

Easter

Age range
Five to eleven.

Group size
Any.

What you need
Photocopiable page 121.

What to do
Easter is a Christian festival celebrating the resurrection of Jesus Christ. Many symbols are linked to this festival, and some, such as the hare, even originate from pagan times. Symbols such as eggs are part of the idea of new life with the coming of spring and are now joined to the belief in Christ's rebirth.

The word Easter derives from the pre-Christian goddess Eostre. Her festival was celebrated at the spring equinox.

The design on photocopiable page 121 could be used as a heading or as a notice for a special assembly, Easter play, egg decorating contest or Easter bonnet parade. It could also be used to make greetings cards, Easter baskets, worksheets and displays. The cross and candle are symbolic of the Christian Church and can be used for a multitude of purposes linked to work on Christianity. They are particularly relevant to the Easter festival and would be useful in much the same way as the specific Easter designs.

Harvest Festival

Age range
Five to eleven.

Group size
Any.

What you need
Photocopiable page 121.

What to do
Organised Harvest Festivals celebrated in church are relatively new, dating from Victorian times. However, for centuries people have given thanks for the food they have successfully grown.

This festival can be celebrated by making displays of goods brought in by the children and then distributing these to elderly people locally.

The simple 'harvest' design on photocopiable page 121 can be used as a heading for children's work, written or pictorial. This could include things like invitations to a harvest celebration, lists of food grown in Britain, food which has to be imported, the children's favourite foods, the story of bread and so on.

Saint Nicholas

Age range
Six to eleven.

Group size
Individuals, small groups or whole class.

What you need
Photocopiable page 122.

What to do
St Nicholas is the patron saint of children and of a number of countries including Russia. He was a well-loved bishop who lived in the fourth century in what is now called Turkey.

Many customs have since grown up around St Nicholas, and St Nicholas's day is celebrated on 6 December and is especially popular in Holland.

Saint Nicholas is thought to be the person on whom Father Christmas is based. He helped many people, including three sisters who were about to be sold into slavery by their impoverished parents. He gave each of them some gold, ensuring that they could afford to buy their freedom. The symbol of the three balls of gold is used by moneylenders and pawnbrokers as their trademark.

Photocopiable page 122 shows pictures of St Nicholas and Father Christmas. These illustrations can be used as headings for worksheets or to make greetings cards, mobiles, displays and stand-up models. For the mobiles and models, photocopy the illustrations on to stiff card.

Christmas

Age range
Four to eleven.

Group size
Individuals or groups.

What you need
Photocopiable page 123.

What to do
The various designs shown on photocopiable page 123 can be used in many ways for the Christmas festival. The 'Dickensian' style shops can be used as borders for worksheets, invitations, greetings cards and handbills or joined together to make a border for a main title on a display. The holly design can be used in much the same way.

Other possible ways of using these pictures are as follows:
● Christmas bookmarks (by photocopying them on to brightly coloured card);
● gift tags (by folding the pictures in half);
● strips to decorate party hats;
● place mats;
● name labels;
● advent calendars;
● Christmas crackers;
● Christmas stockings and tree decorations.

The 'Merry Christmas' illustration on photocopiable page 123 can be photocopied on to stiff card which is twice the size of the illustration and then folded in half to make a greetings card. It can also be used as a heading for story or poem sheets and handbills.

Jewish festivals

Age range
Five to eleven.

Group size
Any.

What you need
Photocopiable page 124 and any other relevant information needed.

What to do
There are many important Jewish festivals during the Jewish lunar calendar, which include the following:
- Hannukah (Festival of Lights). This festival celebrates the lighting of the temple lamp in Jerusalem after it was recaptured from the Syrians about 2000 years ago. It is celebrated in December and Jewish families traditionally light a candle each evening which is placed in the menorah candlestick.
- Succot. This is the Jewish feast of the tabernacles, which celebrates the gathering of the harvest and remembers how the Israelites lived for 40 years in the desert, after escaping from Egypt. It normally falls during September or October.
- Pesach (Passover). This festival occurs during March or April and celebrates the Israelites' escape from slavery in Egypt. It is a time when Jews remember Moses and the plagues that 'passed over' Jewish homes, but affected the Egyptians.
- Rosh Hashanah. This festival celebrates the Jewish New Year and occurs during September or October. Yom Kippur or the Day of Atonement follows on the tenth day after Rosh Hashanah. Yom Kippur is the

holiest day in the Jewish year, when Jews fast for twenty-four hours, pray and ask God for forgiveness.

The designs on photocopiable page 124 are generally appropriate to any work on Judaism. The 'Star of David' is a well known Jewish symbol and is also known as Solomon's seal. Both David and Solomon were Kings of Israel. David slew Goliath and captured Jerusalem and Solomon was famous for his wisdom and built the temple in Jerusalem.

The menorah candlestick, although especially relevant to Hannukah, is also used widely as a Jewish symbol. The two words in Hebrew are also well known; *shalom* meaning peace and *mazal-tov* meaning good luck and/ or congratulations. The latter is often said at weddings and found on greetings cards, for example, for a Jewish boy or girl's Bar Mitzvah.

Islamic festivals

Age range
Five to eleven.

Group size
Any.

What you need
Photocopiable page 125.

What to do
The Islamic calendar is based on lunar months and so Islamic festivals occur at different times each year. The following are some of the festivals:
● Ramadan. This is a time which reminds Muslims of when the Prophet Mohammed received revelations from God. During this festival, which lasts for thirty days, Muslims must not eat or drink anything between sunrise and sunset, although children and the sick are excluded from this. It is an important time to all Muslims and religious observances are particularly strongly adhered to, reminding Muslims of the importance of submitting to God's will. Ramadan also helps Muslims to appreciate all that God has given them.

● Eid-ul-Fitr. This festival comes at the end of Ramadan. It is a happy occasion when special meals are prepared, new clothes worn, visits made to family and friends, and presents given to children. The date for Eid-ul-Fitr varies each year, but can be checked on a calendar.
● Eid-ul-Adha. This is the festival when Muslims remember when Abraham was ready to sacrifice his son on God's orders. By celebrating this festival, Muslims show that they are willing to give up things dear to them for God.

Photocopiable page 125 shows the Islamic symbol of the crescent moon with a star; the Arabic word *Allah*, which means God, and some patterns based on Islamic designs. Islam does not allow images of people or animals, but instead intricate geometric patterns are used alongside beautifully scripted words from the Qu'ran (holy book).

Children could try to design their own patterns based on different shapes or flowers. All the designs on photocopiable page 125 are appropriate for any work on Islam in school and can be used as borders for written work or display material and work about the various festivals and customs.

Allah

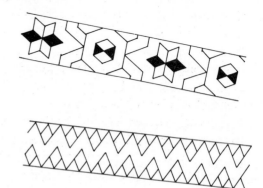

Sikh festivals

Age range
Five to eleven.

Group size
Any.

What you need
Photocopiable pages 126 and other relevant information if needed.

What to do
Sikhs use the same lunar calendar as Hindus, which means that many festivals are not celebrated on fixed dates, but follow the phases of the moon. During the year Sikhs celebrate a number of festivals, including the following:

● The birth of Guru Nanak. This is in November and is the Sikhs' most holy festival. Guru Nanak founded the Sikh religion. The day is celebrated in the Gurudwara (temple), singing holy songs, telling stories and reading the Guru Granth Sahib (holy book).

● Baisakhi. This day falls on 13 April and celebrates the founding of the Sikh brotherhood, the Khalsa, by Guru Gobind Singh. The Khalsa was a Sikh military brotherhood who were totally loyal to their faith. They gave their religion a new strength, while showing compassion and fairness. This festival also marks the start of the Sikh New Year.

● Diwali. This is traditionally a Hindu festival, but it is also celebrated by many Sikhs. It is the day on which Sikhs remember the release of Guru Har Gobind from prison. It is celebrated by lighting up the Gurudwara, and there are often firework displays too.

● Birth of Guru Gobind Singh. He was the last of the ten Gurus (holy teachers) and was born in 1666. He formed the Khalsa (Sikh brotherhood) and gave the Sikh holy book, the Guru Granth Sahib, its name. The other nine Gurus are: Guru Nanak (1469–1539); Guru Angad (1504–1552); Guru Amar Das (1479–1552); Guru Ram Das (1534–1581); Guru Arjan (1563–1606); Guru Har Gobind (1595–1644); Guru Har Rai (1630–1661); Guru Har Krishan (1656–1664) and Guru Tegh Bahadur (1621–1675).

The illustrations on photocopiable page 126 are flexible in their use and can be used for any work on Sikhism. There is a picture of Guru Nanak, the founder of Sikhism; a simple drawing of the Golden Temple of Amritsar, the Sikhs' holiest place; and the Sikh emblem, the Khanda, showing a circle, two scimitars and a double-edged sword. Sikhs have five personal symbols as a sign of their faith. They are: the kara which is a steel bracelet; the kirpan which is a short sword to be used in self-defence; the kacchehra which are special shorts; kesh which is uncut hair; and the kangha which is a comb fixed into the hair. Male Sikhs also wear turbans to cover their hair.

Hindu festivals

Age range
Five to eleven.

Group size
Any.

What you need
Photocopiable page 127.

What to do
There are many different gods and goddesses in the Hindu religion, but most Hindus believe that there is in fact one Supreme God and that the other gods and goddesses represent the various 'faces' and characteristics of this one God.

The three pictures on photocopiable page 127 show the goddess Lakshmi, the god Ganesh and the holy word 'Om'. Lakshmi is the goddess of good fortune. She is often worshipped at Diwali as this festival marks the New Year in many parts of India and it is hoped she will bring success during the coming year. Ganesh, the elephant-headed god, is popular and cheerful. He is the Lord of Obstacles and his worshippers pray for him to remove or solve any problems they may encounter. He is also connected with scholarly pursuits. He is often represented and worshipped at the beginning of an important time in life; for example, he is often pictured on wedding invitations. 'Om' is the sacred word and is the Hindu symbol for the whole of creation and of spiritual good. It is often chanted in prayer. Many Hindus have this word in some form in their homes, for example, as a poster.

There are many Hindu festivals, for example the following:

● Diwali. This is the Festival of Lights and falls in October or November. It celebrates the return of King Rama and his wife Sita after a 14 year exile from their kingdom. The idea of light over darkness, good conquering evil, is very much a part of Diwali and so lights such as diva lamps form an integral part of the celebrations.

Diwali is also a time to offer prayers to the goddess Lakshmi, the bringer of fortune and wealth.

The Hindu New Year starts straight after Diwali and is a time for new ventures and sorting out problems and disagreements.

● Holi. This is a spring festival falling in March. The themes central to this festival are colour and fire. Bonfires are lit with the idea of burning last year's rubbish and starting afresh, and red powder or paint is thrown. The whole festival is great fun!

● Raksha Bandhan. This is the day in July or August, when sisters honour their brothers. They tie bands around their brothers' wrists to show their love and respect. The brothers return the honour by assuring protection for their sisters and often they mark their foreheads with red powder.

All the designs on photocopiable page 127 can be used to illustrate worksheets or as headings for pieces of work. They can also be enlarged to become part of a display on some aspect of Hinduism, such as a particular festival. Lakshmi and Ganesh could be photocopied on to card which can then be folded double, coloured and cut out leaving a join, so making stand-up cards or models, or they could be used as part of a mobile or for decoration.

Chinese New Year

Age range
Five to eleven.

Group size
Any.

What you need
Photocopiable page 128.

What to do
The most important festival for the Chinese is the Spring Festival which marks the New Year. The Chinese calendar is based on lunar months and so the date of this celebration varies, but it is usually during January or February. The festival involves preparing special foods, wearing new clothes, giving gifts, visiting family and friends, decorating homes and places of work and sending cards.

The Lantern Festival starts after the two-week Spring Festival and as its name implies, everywhere is decorated with lanterns. At this time, the well-known dragon and lion street dances take place. Both of these festivals celebrate the coming of the New Year.

Photocopiable page 128 shows two designs and the phrase 'Kung Hai Fat Choy' meaning Happy New Year. They can be used to make greetings cards, to decorate lanterns or gift envelopes, to illustrate children's written work or as part of a larger display. Chinese New Year cards normally have a red background and the gift envelopes are also red, decorated in gold and quite small in size, rather like small wage envelopes.

Children are always fascinated to know about the names of each year, which are on a twelve-year cycle, each of the years being represented by an animal: Rat (1972/1984), Ox (1973/1985), Tiger (1974/1986), Hare (1975/1987), Dragon (1976/1988), Snake (1977/1989), Horse (1978/1990), Ram (1979/1991), Monkey (1980/1992), Cockerel (1981/1993), Dog (1982/1994), Pig (1983/1995) and back to Rat.

Birthdays, see page 99

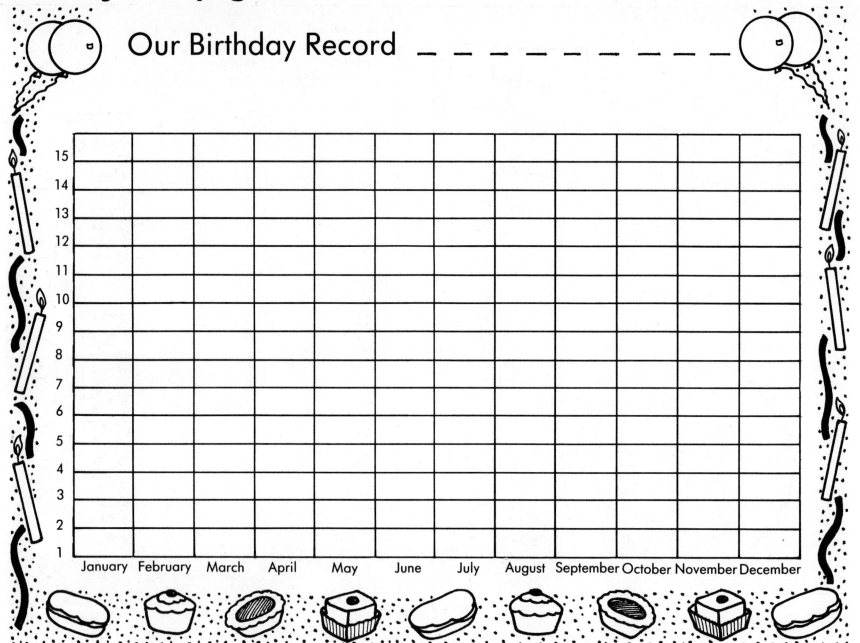

Our Birthday Record _ _ _ _ _ _ _ _ _

	January	February	March	April	May	June	July	August	September	October	November	December
15												
14												
13												
12												
11												
10												
9												
8												
7												
6												
5												
4												
3												
2												
1												

Happy Birthday

Best wishes

It's my birthday

Happy Birthday

to

from

Commonwealth Day and Remembrance Sunday, see pages 102 and 103

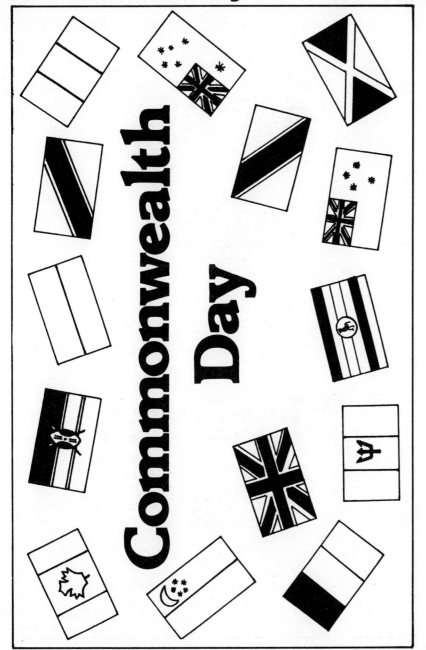

This page may be photocopied for use in the classroom and should not be declared in any return in respect of any photocopying licence.

All Fools' Day

St Valentine's Day

Easter

Harvest

St Nicholas

Christmas, see page 108

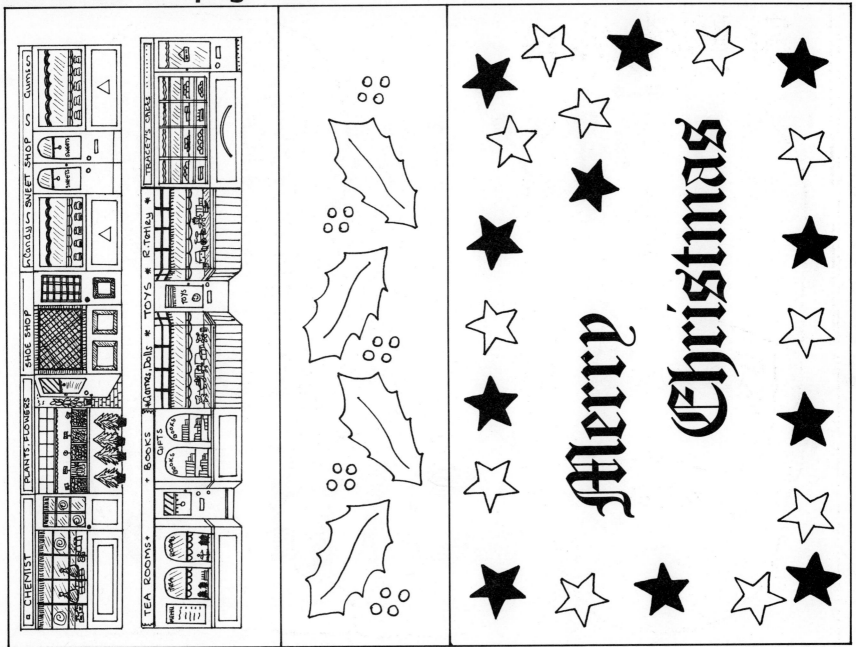

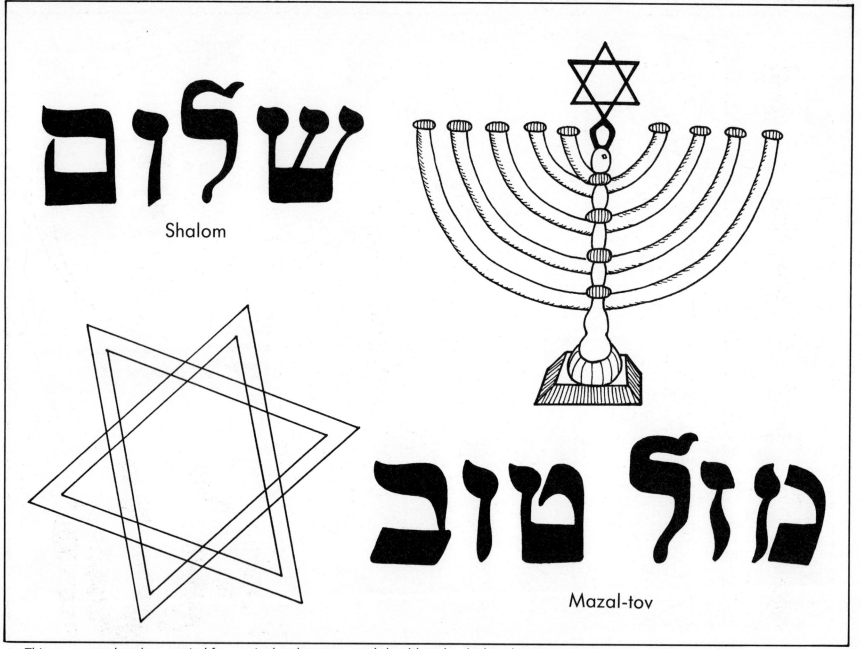

שָׁלוֹם

Shalom

מַזָל טוֹב

Mazal-tov

Allah

Sikh festivals, see page 111

Hindu festivals, see page 112

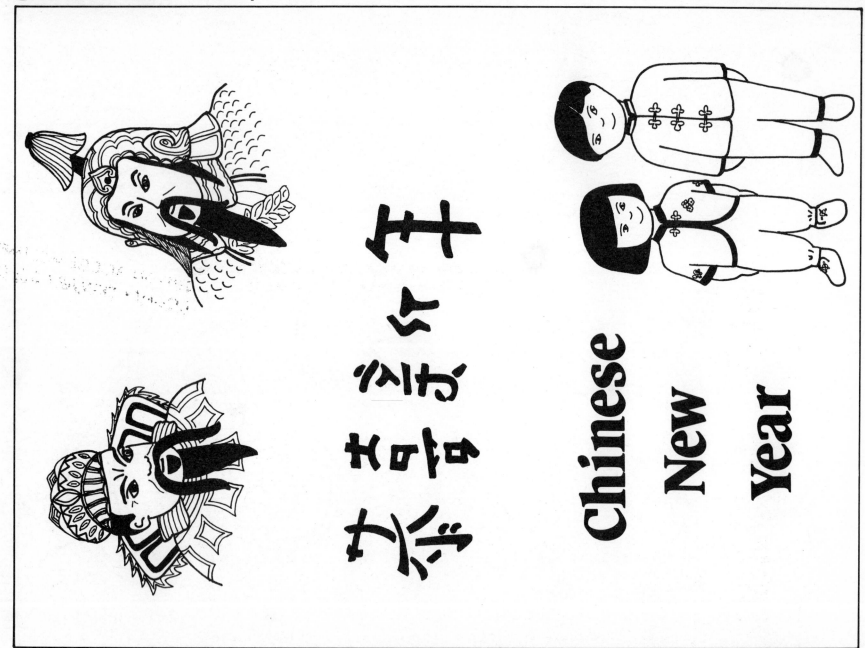